LEGACIES
OF ANTI-SEMITISM IN FRANCE

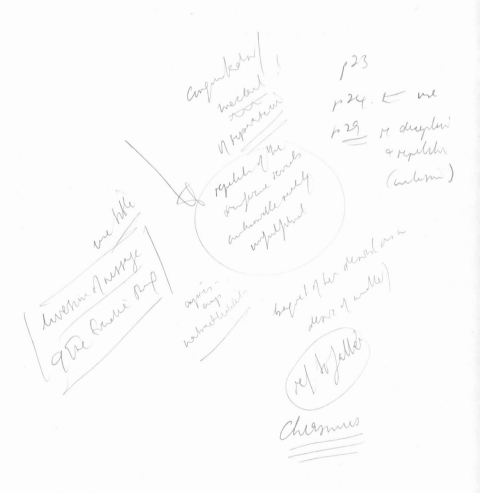

The University of Minnesota Press
gratefully acknowledges assistance provided
by the McKnight Foundation
for publication of this book.

LEGACIES

OF
ANTI-SEMITISM
IN FRANCE

JEFFREY MEHLMAN

UNIVERSITY OF MINNESOTA PRESS, MINNEAPOLIS

Library of Congress Cataloging in Publication Data

Mehlman, Jeffrey.
    Legacies: Of anti-Semitism in France.

    Includes bibliographical references and index.
    1. Anti-Semitism — France — History — Addresses, essays,
lectures. 2. Jews in literature — Addresses, essays,
lectures. 3. France — Intellectual life — Addresses, essays,
lectures. 4. France — Ethnic relations — Addresses,
essays, lectures. I. Title.
DS146.F8M44 1983   944'.004924   83-3685
ISBN 0-8166-1177-7
ISBN 0-8166-1178-5 (pbk.)

In memory of my mother

and

For Alicia, Natalia, and my father

absurdis interpretationibus seipsos tradentes

—Justinian, *Novella CXLVI, De Hebraeis*

I would like to thank

the John Simon Guggenheim Memorial Foundation,

whose generosity allowed me

to complete this book.

—J. M.

TABLE OF CONTENTS

Introduction   *3*

   I. Blanchot at *Combat*:
     Of Literature and Terror   *6*

  II. The Suture of an Allusion:
     Lacan with Léon Bloy   *23*

 III. A Future for *Andromaque*:
     Aryan and Jew in Giraudoux's France   *34*

 IV. "Jewish Literature"
     and the Art of André Gide   *64*

Conclusion   *83*

Appendix I   *93*

Appendix II   *107*

Notes   *113*

Index of Names   *139*

LEGACIES
OF ANTI-SEMITISM IN FRANCE

INTRODUCTION

The four essays in this book—on Blanchot, Lacan, Giraudoux, and Gide—are linked by a common temporal disjunction at their core. On the one hand, they concern writers important and recent enough to figure, however differently, as our virtual contemporaries.[1] On the other, each of those writers is separated from us, radically, by the fact that a crucial period of his life and work was pursued prior to—and in innocence of—the grisly culmination of a series of ideological and political wagers in the events of World War II. Specifically, it is Hitler's liquidation of anti-Semitism as a tenable option for a French intellectual that forms the pivot of this work.[2] And the strangeness of these pages lies principally in their effort to extrapolate from a series of barely imaginable points of tangency with that dissipated—or dormant—tradition readings of authors who, each in his way, have provided the very parameters of our imaginative and interpretive possibilities.[3] It is within this temporal disjunction, then, that I have attempted to write what should perhaps be thought of less as a marginal chapter in the sorry history of anti-Semitism in France than four practical contributions to a political aesthetic of *Verfremdung*.

These pages, then, are exploratory rather than accusatory. Indeed as the analyses engage such crucial questions as the inaugural silence in Blanchot's sense of literature, the "style" of Lacan, the relation to Racine of Giraudoux, and the sexual politics of Gide, it will be perceived that the readings are ultimately less dependent on any category of intentionality than on the sustaining effects of a cultural *milieu* that at times seems—or seemed—anti-Jewish in its essence. As in the Jewish joke that has a German in 1942 inquire untranslatably of a young man in Paris, "où se trouve la place de l'Etoile?," only to find his interlocutor

3

gesturing in response to his left lapel.[4] It is as though only the slightest displacement were necessary within the designation of the French monument to reveal therein a drama of Jewish exclusion. I have attempted, in four cases, such a displacement, aware that in the long run it is the degree of coherence of the readings proposed that will—or will not—justify the effort.

There is a sense in which the monumental and monstrous case of Céline has constituted the resistance against which the perceptions of this book were registered. For the exceptional instance of a genius gone mad with anti-Jewish rage risks blinding us to a sustaining anti-Semitism which, less flamboyantly, at times appears to be the medium of French cultural achievement at its most characteristic . . . and "humane." It is one thing, for example, for L. Poliakov, in his *Histoire de l'antisémitisme*, to reproduce a truculent paragraph by the racist ethnographer Vacher de Lapouge, and posit—convincingly—Céline's debt to his writing.[5] It is another, however, to gauge the significance of Paul Valéry's patient apprenticeship at Vacher's side in 1891, measuring the dimensions of 600 skulls exhumed from a disaffected Montpellier cemetery.[6] Hovering in its ideality over contemporary French poetry's crowning—and most sober—achievement, "Le cimetière marin," what indeed *is* a "tête complète et parfait diadème," and what the series of associations radiating throughout Valéry's poetry from it?[7] Although I have not written of the author of *Monsieur Teste* in this volume, it is problems of the sort raised by his (implicit) relation to Vacher, rather than Céline's, that have interested me.[8] Ultimately, that is, my subject in each essay has been the disturbing repercussions of a lost pre-World War II sensibility in our postwar sense of cultural achievement. Although the events of the war constitute something of a pivot, in themselves they are not the focus of this work.[9]

These introductory remarks are deliberately fragmentary, even as the four essays maintain their discreteness. For in matters as volatile as these, every move toward synthesis runs the risk of effacing the thin barrier between legitimate interpretation and paranoia of a particularly sensationalistic sort.[10] The infinitesimal quality of that distinction was, of course, a concern of Freud's, whose lesson on these matters I have attempted to respect. Indeed it is under the aegis of the later Freud—and his liberating articulation of repetition, interpretation, and masochism—that I would place this book, as I have my others. In the world of textual analysis, we are still hard put to move beyond *Beyond the Pleasure Principle*.

* * *

Gershom Scholem, in one of his laments on the delusions governing speculations on the possibility of a "German-Jewish dialogue," observes that the term "Jew" in postwar Germany had little reality other than as an embarrassing reminder of anti-Semitic contempt.[11] Paradoxically, the term "anti-Semite" in our Western democracies has come, since the war, to be little more than a term of liberal abuse. That latter situation perhaps offers some limited consolation for the horrors that culminated in the former. But it constitutes as well an inhibition on understanding that I have attempted, with some anxiety, in four limited cases, to raise.

I.

BLANCHOT AT *COMBAT:*
OF LITERATURE AND TERROR

Shortly after the death of Maurice Clavel, Michel Foucault was moved
to interrupt a page of tribute with an eloquent digression whose tension he seemed uninterested in resolving: "Blanchot: diaphanous, immobile, awaiting a day more transparent than light, attentive to the
signs that signal only in the movement that effaces them. Clavel: impatient, bounding at the slightest noise, crying out at twilight, calling
forth the storm. These men—could any two be more different?—have
introduced into the world without orient in which we live the sole
tension that will not eventually leave us embarrassed—or amused: one
that rents the fabric of time."[1] If ours—or his—be the age of Blanchot
and Clavel, to sketch a history that integrates them in their apparent
difference is perhaps to contribute to an understanding of the life of
the mind in France in the last half-century. Such is the horizon of the
analysis—or narrative—that follows.

I

Our point of departure is the series of talks Georges Bernanos delivered
to the royalist youth of Action française in 1929. Those lectures eventually grew into Bernanos's first major political volume, *La Grande
Peur des bien-pensants* (1931).[2] Its purpose: to transmit to a new
generation of Frenchmen the lost heritage of radical anti-Semitism in
the form of a biography in praise of Edouard Drumont. Drumont's *La
France juive* (1886), more than a thousand pages long, attempted to
found left-wing (anticapitalist) anti-Semitism as *the* philosophy of
French modernity, to rewrite Taine's *Conquête jacobine* as *La Conquête juive*.[3] His book, along with Renan's *Vie de Jésus*, was one of

the two best-selling enterprises of the second half of the nineteenth century in France, and indeed, reading the reactions of French politicians at the mobilizing force of anti-Semitism during the last years of that century, one has the feeling that they too felt they had stumbled on to something larger in significance than even their own cynicism could encompass.[4] It was as though anti-Semitism—and not the general strike—would be the great myth (in the sense that Georges Sorel was concurrently elaborating) of the burgeoning twentieth century.[5]

What is the organization of Bernanos's *Grande Peur*? Briefly: In an act of printed insurrection against the wholesale liquidation of public decency in Republican France, Drumont risks everything in his immense book on Jewish capitalism and the corrupt and all but totalitarian domination in which it holds France. His great enemy: the diabolical Clemenceau, the man who had just dragged Bernanos's France through the deceptions of a world war, completing the disintegration of the values of "la vieille France." Drumont's ally, or rather his heir apparent: an *enfant terrible* named the Marquis de Morès. Morès was a flamboyant aristocrat who had gone off to North Dakota to organize his own cattle empire and still figures as a brutal hero of American Western mythology.[6] In Paris, he had organized the butchers of La Villette into an anti-Semitic gang, and in his writings advocated a fusion of syndicalism with the anti-Semitic movement, a project he called in 1894 "la doctrine du faisceau."[7] It is the earliest reference to fascism I have been able to locate.

In Bernanos's plot, Clemenceau deviously exploits the weakness of Morès, arranges for a loan through a Jewish financier to this desperate gambler down on his luck, and then publishes the fact in *L'Aurore*. Morès, that is, is a historical prototype for Bernanos's subsequent *enfants humiliés*, and will go off, caught up in what the author would later thematize as *imposture* (and Lacan as *l'imaginaire*), on a suicidal colonial venture to North Africa, where he is in fact murdered by a member of his party.[8] The whole of Bernanos's subsequent analysis— and condemnation—of Hitler is already present in the self-destructive venture of Morès, *enfant humilié*, but for our purposes I shall merely insist that what was at stake in *La Grande Peur* for the author was finding a new generation to take up the concerns of the hero of his youth, Drumont, and, presumably, replacing the fallen theorist of the *faisceau*, Morès.[9] And indeed the review *Réaction* was organized around and sustained a cult for Bernanos's "life and times" of Drumont.[10]

Bernanos incarnated as well a second heritage, that of the Cercle Proudhon of 1913: a fusion of antidemocrats from the Action française and from Sorelian syndicalism that had been snuffed out by the great war and that was being mythologized, by the 1930s, as the first fascist organization in Europe.[11] Bernanos, in *Les Grands Cimetières sous la lune* (1938), on his youth in the Action française: "We were not right-wingers [*des gens de droite*]. The group for social studies we had founded bore the name Cercle Proudhon, flaunted that scandalous affiliation. Our hopes were with syndicalism, which was then just emerging. . . . In the prison of La Santé, where we periodically checked in, we shared our provisions fraternally with laborers; we sang alternately *Vive Henri IV* and the *Internationale*. Drumont was still alive at the time, and there is not a single line of this book that he could not have signed with his hand."[12] Drieu la Rochelle (1934): "it will be seen that several elements of the fascist atmosphere were already united in France toward 1913 before they were elsewhere. There were young men, coming from different social classes, who were animated by the love of heroism and violence and who dreamed of fighting what they called evil on two fronts: capitalism and parliamentary socialism, and reclaiming what was their own from both sides. There were, I believe, at Lyon men who called themselves socialist-royalists or something similar. Already the marriage of nationalism and socialism was projected. Yes, in France, in the vicinity of the Action Française and Péguy, there was the nebula of a kind of fascism."[13]

It has recently been demonstrated, in a scrupulous investigation of the "French origins of fascism," just how astonishingly much of French political culture reached its culmination in the Cercle Proudhon.[14] But in the present context, I would simply insist on the dual heritage that Bernanos, even as he began abandoning it, represented in the 1930s. And on its transmission. Thierry Maulnier, heir apparent to Maurras, founded in 1937 the weekly *L'Insurgé*, under the joint patronage of Vallès and Drumont.[15] And from 1936 to 1939 he codirected an important monthly, *Combat*, that seemed intent on reviving the tradition of "Fascisme 1913," as a lead article called it.[16] Periodically, the journal featured pages of pedagogically selected excerpts from authors worth rereading. Prominent among them were Drumont, Maurras, and Sorel.

Enter Maurice Blanchot. In a guise barely recognizable: leading contributor of political articles to *Combat*.[17] From 1936 to 1938, that is, Blanchot appears not as a *littérateur* with "rightist" leanings, but essentially as a political thinker in an enterprise central to his generation: "the final stage, the point of arrival of the young Right," in the retrospective view of P. Andreu, a leading contributor.[18] I have been able to locate and read the *Combat* articles, and I would like in what follows to sketch a hypothetical path — or series of paths — through Blanchot's writing to the very different incarnation that has figured so centrally for a generation of literary critics.

In November 1936, Blanchot published "La Grande Passion des modérés."[19] Here then was a text positioned explicitly within the wake of *La Grande Peur*. The Bernanosian theme of the gutlessness of the Right, the abdication of the French elite, is sounded with a violence worth savoring. The subject is the alibi that the French Right has found for its own cowardice in the "simulacrum" of "neutrality" the French Republic had instituted with respect to the Spanish Civil War: "And it is here that we encounter the right-wingers [*des gens de droite*]. It should be acknowledged that today's moderates have made progress. Yesterday they would have condemned with horror the violence of an insurrection directed against the government forces. They would have wailed and rejected, deplorably, any risk of being compromised by that frightful brawl. You would have seen them dig their way like rats into the holes of integral neutrality. It was the time when moderates still dared to appear moderate. Today, we find something quite different. Those unfortunates, who disperse with every draft of air, having passed three-quarters of their life commuting impotently between two excesses, have discovered the usefulness of force. Every day they comically invent new chiefs, and, as soon as they think they detect an autocrat on the horizon, throw themselves deliriously at his feet. It's the latest thrill [*le frisson nouveau*]. Mussolini's bronze pout has them swooning. The monotone howls of Hitler leave them frightened and ravished, as after a few slightly strong obscenities. And now, what luck to have Franco. . . . It is thus that every morning and every evening, at the hour of the *communiqué*, a certain number of comfortably ensconced Frenchmen grow jubilant upon learning that Spain is being forged anew midst ruin and bloodshed. . . . We believe quite simply that that state of soul is disgusting."[20] If Blanchot here mocks the French Right's allegiance to Franco as feigned, Bernanos, of course, would later attack Franco as a bogus Primo de Rivera.[21] But

what is striking in the passage quoted is its exacerbation of a charac-
teristically Bernanosian combination of *machismo* and disgust at the
abdications of the Right at a time when "a band of degenerates and
traitors"—read: Léon Blum and the Front populaire—"dishonors the
country without resistance."

An initial exposure to the verbal violence of the first Blanchot is
perhaps useful in conveying to the reader just what an enigma the career of Blanchot constitutes. The link with Bernanos is more subtle,
however. What both share is a sense of the system of representation—
the Republic—as astonishing in the systematicity of its failures. Thus
Bernanos, in *La Grande Peur*, discussing his "surprise" at "the blun-
dering impotence of our respectable citizens [*honnêtes gens*], the astonishing dupery which has them starting out as invokers or preachers
of the greater good only to end up, invariably, by a kind of harsh and
comic fatality, as servants of the greater evil."[22] Now the general structure of Blanchot's political articles in *Combat* offers, on the one hand,
a series of depictions of just such an infernal—or comic—machine (in
the systematicity with which it thwarts itself), and, on the other, a sequence of increasingly strident calls to acts of violence against the
regime.

Take, for example, Blanchot's comments on the Geneva doctrine
(the League of Nations) after the German reoccupation of the Rhine-
land in 1936: "That mad and ostentatious machine has succeeded in
unleashing a mechanism [*engrenage*] in which every valid thing that
has been accomplished on behalf of the peace as well as everything
baneful perpetrated against it are engaged. . . . All of our treaties are
grafted on to the Geneva pact. There is nothing more demanding and
more feeble, more harmful and, in appearance, more necessary than
the League of Nations. It seems equally impossible to leave it and to
remain within it . . ."[23] The impotence of French political life is a
function of its being caught up in a diabolical series of irreducible con-
tradictions. The France Blanchot detests seems immobilized in the
paradoxes his articles castigate. Thus the "simulacrum of neutrality"
behind which the French Right paraded during the Spanish Civil War
takes on a reality. It effectively serves as a justification for a certain
non-intervention. But France itself, in an article entitled "La France,
nation à venir," has discovered its vocation in a generalized paralysis:
"This country . . . employs all its ingenuity in abstaining and appearing not to abstain. This is an absolute rule. . . . It will at last be

seen to what an extent, during this period, France has been unreal [*ir-réelle*]."[24] That is, even as the simulacrum of neutrality has begun taking on a certain positivity, France itself has lapsed into irreality, become the mere occasion of some future "France à venir."

The solution: a renewal of the insurrection of February 6, 1934, or, failing that, acts of terrorism.[25] Two examples follow.

> The shameful Sarraut government, which seems to have received the mission of humiliating France as it had not been humiliated in twenty-five years, has driven this disorder to a pitch. It has said everything that should not have been said; it has done nothing of what should have been done. It began by hearing the appeals of unfettered revolutionaries and Jews, whose theological furor demanded against Hitler all possible sanctions immediately. Nothing could be as dangerous or senseless as that delirium of verbal energy. Nothing could be as perfidious as that propaganda for national honor, executed by foreigners suspected by the offices of the Quai d'Orsay, to precipitate young Frenchmen, in the name of Moscow or Israel, into an immediate conflict. A day will come when it will be necessary to search out those responsible for this frenzy that could lead us only to adventurism or surrender. Already today, three men are identified: Sarraut, Flandin, Mandel will pay for the risk to which they exposed the peace, and they will pay for the dishonor through which they subsequently attempted to elude that risk.[26]

> It is necessary that there be a revolution because one does not modify a regime which controls everything, which has its roots everywhere. One removes it, one strikes it down. It is necessary that that revolution be violent because one does not tap a people as enervated [*aveuli*] as our own for the strength and passions appropriate to a regeneration through measures of decency, but through a series of bloody shocks, a storm that will overwhelm—and thus awaken—it. This is not a totally secure undertaking [*cela n'est pas de tout repos*], but precisely what is needed is a failure of security. That is why terrorism at present appears to us as a method of public salvation [*comme une méthode de salut public*].[27]

Our second specimen, moreover, is excerpted from an article predicated against "the detestable character of what is called, with solemnity, the Blum experiment."

II

Now the first text that Blanchot publishes in a separate format on a literary subject is a short pamphlet of 1942 entitled "Comment la littérature est-elle possible?"[28] It was adapted from articles contributed to the *Journal des débats* and was later incorporated in part as something of a centerpiece in *Faux pas* (1943). Oddly enough, its focus is a different terrorism and, dare I say, a different bloom: Jean Paulhan's *Les Fleurs de Tarbes ou la Terreur dans les lettres*.

Paulhan's book can be read, Blanchot suggests, as an admirable essay in neoclassical aesthetics, a dismantling of that terror against *flowers* of rhetoric that gives the book its title. But might there not be as well a second reading, far more radical, invited by Paulhan's concluding "words of retraction," and opening on to a secret: "an infernal machine which, invisible today, will one day explode, overwhelming literature [*les lettres*] and rendering its use impossible"?[29] Such is Blanchot's query, and he answers in the affirmative. That infernal machine is perhaps best understood in terms of contemporary deconstruction, the heritage of the style of reading Blanchot was then initiating. Terrorism is an incipient logocentrism exercised against language insofar as it is thinkable as debased repetition: what Paulhan calls *clichés*, what has been more generally thematized as *écriture*. Exploiting an inherent duplicity in *cliché*, Blanchot brings his reading of Paulhan to the point where Terror—the search for the discursive equivalent of "virgin contact" with reality, the "soul" of literature—has as its enabling condition that which it is predicated against: "It is a matter of revealing to the writer that he gives birth to art only through a vain and blind struggle against it, that the work he believes he has reclaimed [*arraché*] from ordinary or vulgar language exists due to the vulgarization of virginal language, through an additional dose of impurity and debasement . . . he writes only through the help of what he detests."[30]

The future of French criticism wrested from Paulhan's text by Blanchot in 1942: logocentrism local in an economy of language-as-repetition (*cliché*)? But what if we were to read the Blanchot-Paulhan encounter in the spirit in which Blanchot reads Paulhan, following "several hesitant allusions" to a *different* enigma?[31] Blanchot would perhaps have us do as much: "once one has learned to read this book, one realizes that one knows how to read almost all the others . . ."[32] Wherefore consider:

1. The key to the "infernal machine" in Paulhan is his word of retraction at the end, says Blanchot. At the conclusion of *Faux pas*, discussing *Solstice de juin*, the volume that earned Montherlant his accusation as a collaborator, Blanchot quotes approvingly Montherlant's

observations on writers lost in politics: "To writers who have given too much these last months to recent events [*l'actualité*], I predict, for that part of their work, total oblivion. When I open the newspapers, the journals of today, I can hear rolling over them the indifference of the future, as one hears the sound of the sea upon lifting certain seashells to one's ear."[33] Plainly, this concluding "retraction" is Blanchot bidding farewell to his political career as . . . a propagandist for terrorism.

2. The Terror of Paulhan found its philosopher, he tells us, in Henri Bergson.[34] Indeed, the mythic efficacy of the Terror is indistinguishable from the influence of Bergson's philosophy.[35] But behind *Combat*'s calls to terrorism were the Sorelian politics of violence of the Cercle Proudhon.[36] And the heart of the *Réflexions sur la violence* lay in an attempted wedding of Marx with Bergson.[37]

3. The examples of clichés against which Paulhan's Terror operates happen to be *liberté, démocratie, ordre*. So writes Blanchot in 1942.[38]

4. Finally, Blanchot concludes his exposition of Paulhan's infernal machine: "There is in that discovery enough to cause the silence of Rimbaud to descend on all."[39] At the inception of a certain literary modernity, that is, there is a radical falling silent.

In a polemical moment Michel Foucault, in dialogue with Gilles Deleuze, wrote: "Secrets are perhaps more difficult to undo [*lever*] than the unconscious. The two themes frequently encountered as recently as yesterday, 'writing is the repressed' and 'writing is of itself subversive', appear to me to betray a certain number of maneuvers that should be severely denounced."[40] Without joining Foucault in his polemic, we are nevertheless hard pressed not to see in the silence at the inception of Blanchot's conception of literature an obliterated part of his own bibliography: the political writings of the 1930s.

"Comment la littérature est-elle possible?" may thus be read simultaneously as a discreet inauguration of French literary modernity and a coded farewell to plans for a French fascism in the 1930s. As the cliché-ridden "infernal machine" absorbs and disarticulates the terrorism that would demolish it, a dream of *action française* gives way to the infinite passivity—"une passivité au-delà de toute passivité"—of *l'espace littéraire*.[41]

III

The division within the esoteric value of "terrorism"—incipient "logocentrism"/the politics of *Combat*—may be profitably linked to the solar mythology latent in *Faux pas*. *Solstice de juin*, for instance, takes its title from a moment of reversal—or decline—in the solar cycle: "June solstice, ambiguous instant, marked by a kind of deception, how it troubles, irritates, pleases me. For months, the year will still appear to mount toward its zenith of heat and splendor, and yet all is over: the days have begun to grow shorter. The sun has inclined; the sun is dying."[42] The solstice, that is, is the moment of return, reversal, repetition which gives the lie to an illusion of ascendant visibility or heat: repetition as the blind spot within phenomenology. But the solstice of 1940 was the date of the armistice signed by Pétain: what is reversed is the result of World War I, as history reveals itself to be cyclical. Now that cyclical structure authorizes a politics of collaboration. For, on the one hand, history at its most sublime converges with sport: "In the evening, the vanquished dine at the victor's table."[43] And on the other, the very symbol of the triumphant solar cycle has a specific contemporary valence: "A week has passed, and today the armistice was signed. June 24. For the summer solstice. The Swastika [*croix gammée*], which is the Solar Wheel, triumphs in one of the sun's revels."[44] The Franco-German cycle, that is, is subsumed by the emblem of Hitler triumphant. But this entire development is the stuff of the call to oblivion—or silence—on which *Faux pas* concludes.[45]

In an earlier chapter of *Faux pas*, "Le Mythe de Phèdre," Blanchot encounters again the combination of darkness at the heart of light and the imperative of silence. The subject is *Lecture de Phèdre* by Thierry Maulnier, cofounder of *L'Insurgé* and coeditor of *Combat*. Blanchot's discussion in 1943 (of Maulnier) has Phèdre as "a supreme offense to the light of day. She is like the very darkness which, without appearing, decomposes light. . . . Phèdre can indeed withdraw into the shadows to restore to daylight its clarity [*rendre au jour sa clarté*], but the day she leaves behind her is a devasted, hollow day."[46] With the inversion at the core of day, moreover, comes, as in *Solstice de juin*, a certain repetition: "The development of the tragedy takes place around an unmoving Phèdre. . . . Delivered over to her alone, it ceaselessly turns away from action, from history . . ."[47] Finally, the entire configuration is the vehicle of a certain muteness at the heart of literature. "That Phèdre's is the tragedy of silence should perhaps be recalled when one is astonished at Racine's silence after *Phèdre*. . . . Phèdre is there to recall the meaning of silence and to confess, along with her own ruin, the effacement of the mind that sought to utilize her to understand the night. Even as she vanishes in a death that is almost serene in its transcendence of the torments of ordinary misfortune, it is natural that she seem to drag along with her he who touched the mystery of what cannot be unveiled and who thereafter can present to the world only its silent incognito."[48] We can easily assemble the motifs of the mute anonymity of the author, the deflection out of historical time, and the irruption of a negative term (darkness) in the heart of the positive opposite that hierarchically governs it as the stuff of what is presently regarded as literary modernity. But consider that the muteness which spreads from "Phèdre" to "Racine" should presumably englobe Blanchot's co-ideologue at *Combat*, Thierry Maulnier, as well. The "silent incognito" that ends the chapter, that is, is superimposable on the appeal to oblivion that ends *Faux pas* itself, or on the "silence of Rimbaud" that Paulhan's discovery would presumably inspire in any would-be terrorist or poet. Which is to say that the whole of the configuration in "Le Mythe de Phédre" is rigorously homologous with the manual of collaboration, *Solstice de juin*, even as it appears a farewell to that eventuality.

A final case of solar mythology in *Faux pas* is the chapter "L'Expérience intérieure," devoted to Bataille. It begins with Nietzsche's invocation of Noontide. Blanchot continues: "The hour of the Great Noon is that which brings us the strongest light; all the air is overheated; the day has become fire; for the man eager to see, it is the moment in which, upon gazing, he risks becoming blinder than a blind man, a kind of seer who remembers the sun as an importunate gray spot."[49] Along with this blindness at the vertex of vision goes a withdrawal from (language as) action: "Communication thus begins to be authentic only when the experience [i.e., *l'expérience intérieure*] has laid bare existence, withdrawn from it what binds it to discourse and action, opened it up to a nondiscursive interiority into which it disappears . . ."[50] And finally, the third term of the configuration, silence considered as what would later be termed double inscription: a work which, "while denouncing itself as the unfaithful depositary (of the experience), doubles its text with another one sustaining and effacing it in a kind of permanent demirefutation."[51] Here then is an early invocation of a "problematic" whose future in France has proved particularly fertile. Yet in *Faux pas* it is inescapably anchored in a series that binds it to the collapse of hopes for a French fascism (Maulnier's "incognito"), the reality of collaboration (Montherlant's *Solstice*), and the obliteration of the political section of Blanchot's bibliography. For it is not by chance that one of the most rigorous discussions of Bataille yet written should begin with a consideration of the Roman ritual performed in preparation for the summer solstice.[52] In brief, *la part du feu*, long opposed in Blanchot to a quasi-Weimarian notion of French clarity, is shot through and through with the historical memory of a political collapse.[53]

IV

Having begun our narrative with Bernanos's attempt to revive and transmit the heritage of radical anti-Semitism, we have come then in Blanchot to the liquidation in *Faux pas* of the general political project drawing on that tradition. For it was in the nature of Hitler's policies to render anti-Semitism a minimally viable alternative in intellectual France.[54] By 1949, Bernanos himself was celebrating in print the heroism of the insurgents of the Warsaw ghetto, meditating on qualities of soul specific to the Jews: "Jewish honor, in fact, for two thousand years, lay in resisting not by force but by patience . . ."[55] Thierry Maulnier, eloquent in 1938 on just how radical a solution the "Jewish problem" would require, authored after the war a panegyric entitled *L'Honneur d'être juif*.[56]

Blanchot's own liquidation of an anti-Semitic past is particularly instructive in another context. Take the short but difficult fictive text *La Folie du jour*, or rather take it in its relation to the commentary it has received from E. Lévinas.[57] The originality of Blanchot's *récit* lies in its articulation of an (anti)metaphysical figure with a political and historical meditation. The title, that is, is readable in terms both of a delirium subverting phenomenology from within and of a contemporary form of insanity. The first motif, termed by Lévinas "the transparency that wounds," brings us back to the solar mythology of *Faux pas*. It entails a blindness in the heart of vision: "I almost lost my sight, someone having crushed some glass against my eyes."[58] An operation to remove the glass follows, but its effect is to institute a new and threatening relation to vision itself: "And if seeing was fire, I required the plenitude of fire, and if seeing was the contagion of madness, I madly desired that madness."[59] In brief, as the transparency (of glass) has entered aggressively into the field of vision, the element of philosophy or theory (Lévinas: "the light that comes to us from

Greece") is scarred: "my sight became a wound [*plaie*]."[60] The glass in the eye is already potentially the knell (*glas*) of philosophy, (Derrida's "Pas," devoted to Blanchot, follows closely his *Glas*), and as such is in communication with the play of darkness irrupting within light whose ramifications in *Faux pas* we began charting.

What of the historico-political dimension of the text: the madness of the *day*? It concerns the institutionalization of the narrator ("I had accepted to let myself be interned").[61] By the end of the text, the reader is left with the impression that everything he or she has heard has been proffered in response to a psychiatric interview, whose coercive nature Blanchot's fragmentarist modernity would be predicated — hopelessly — against: "I noticed then for the first time that they were two, that that violence to traditional method, although explicable by the fact that one was a technician of sight, the other a specialist of mental illness, constantly gave our conversation the character of an authoritarian interrogation, overseen [*surveillé*] and governed by a strict code. Neither one nor the other, to be sure, was the police commissioner. But being two, because of that, they were three, and the third one remained firmly convinced, I am sure, that a writer, a man who speaks and reasons with distinction, is always capable of recounting facts that he remembers. A narrative [*un récit*]? No, no narrative [*pas de récit*], never again."[62] The Heideggerian question, as Lévinas suggests, has lapsed into a police interrogation. The process, moreover, is crucially linked to the relation between blindness and vision. For the narrator finds himself unseeing, but infinitely examined: "And whom did they set up against me? An invisible knowledge that no one could prove . . ."[63] Of the doctors: "I gave them the day. Beneath their totally unmoved eyes, I became a drop of water, an inkspot. I reduced myself to them. I passed entirely within their sight and when at last, having no more to see . . ."[64] The (anti)metaphysical play of darkness at noon, then, can be politicized into the dissymmetry of seeing and (blindly) being seen, the model of hierarchical or disciplinary intensification that Foucault, after Bentham, has called "panoptical."[65] That, no doubt, is why Lévinas, on the one hand, sees *La Folie du jour* as that of a Nazi concentration camp ("Madness of Auschwitz that never comes to pass"), and, on the other, keeps hinting that the true political horizon of Blanchot's 1948 text is the antiauthoritarianism of May 1968.[66] The evocations in the text "do not even reflect the contemporaneity of 1948 at the level of a history of ideas (on this score, *La Folie du jour* would partake rather of 1968)."[67] "A demystification of height after the demystification of the depths. . . . There is in this text of 1948 a troubling premonition of all that was to come to full light and whirl vertiginously [*tournoyer*] midst in-anity and madness, in place, twenty years later."[68]

More than ten years have passed since 1968. Foucault has amplified and generalized his critique of internment into an analysis of a society *panoptical* in its essence. The self-proclaimed heirs of May 1968 have found in Foucault the wherewithal to launch their "new philosophy."[69] In May 1977, Foucault consecrated that "philosophy" in an article in praise of *Les Maîtres Penseurs* of André Glucksmann.[70] Its title: "La Grande Colère des faits."[71] After Blanchot's deliberate invocation of Bernanos's title in "La Grande Passion des modérés," Foucault's offers only the faintest echo. And yet it is strangely appropriate. Foucault: "There, it seems to me, is the center of Glucksmann's book, the fundamental question he is, no doubt, the first to pose: through what turn was German Philosophy able to make of Revolution the promise of a true and good State, and of the State the serene and accomplished form of the Revolution. All of our submissions find their principle in this double inducement: make the Revolution quick, it will give you the State you need; hurry up and make a State, it will generously lavish on you the reasonable effects of the Revolution. Obliged to think the Revolution, beginning and end, the German thinkers pinned it to the State, and designed the State-Revolution, with all of its final solutions. Thus did the master-thinkers [*maîtres penseurs*] implement an entire mental apparatus, the very one subtending the systems of domination and patterns of obedience of modern societies."[72] Leaving aside for a moment the anti-German motif, crucial to French nationalism earlier in the century, we find in Foucault's evocation of Glucksmann a critique of precisely the dangers Bernanos, in the margins of Action française, had castigated in *La Grande Peur des bien-pensants*. For Drumont's discovery, realized in horror at the repression of the Commune, was that the Revolution has been "an enormous imposture." In Bernanos's words, it has always functioned in the service of "a frenetic cult of the state [*un étatisme forcené*]."[73] (Bernanos: "we were not right-wingers [*des gens de droite*] . . .")[74] Indeed, Bernanos's critique of the Statist-Revolution and its heritage casts an eery light on the Foucault-Glucksmann nexus. As though the combination of generalized illegality, discipline, and surveillance Foucault traces to

Bentham's panopticon might have more local roots. Bernanos quotes Drumont: "With the new institution of the 'proletariat,' the bourgeoisie annexed the 'conciergerat,' which our fathers had not known either. The ideal of a well-kept house, in the conciergerat, is a house in which one may commit every turpitude, indulge in every form of debauchery, but in which one does not make any noise, the stairs are adequately waxed, the carpet regularly brushed, and the brass globes vigorously polished, and in which prompt obedience is accorded the plaque reading: 'Kindly Wipe Your Feet.' "[75] Indeed, sex, the ingredient Foucault would later add to the Benthamite model, is already there, profusely, in the passage from Drumont.

The vision on which *Les Maîtres Penseurs* opens is the Abbaye de Thélème as the happy concentration camp, the Nazi project seen as the ultimate realization of centuries of humanism, the telos of Western society. Foucault (ironizing with Glucksmann): "Enter rather into the Abbaye de Thélème; you will be free there, but because you will have been so ordered; you will do what you wish, but the others will do it at the same time as you, and you along with them . . ."[76] This manic version of a concentration camp prepares the central role Glucksmann assigns in history to the Nazi extermination camps (from which, the Goulag). This may bring us back to Lévinas's reading of *la folie du jour* as Auschwitz: "A lucidity more lucid than all lucidity, which, already a state [*déja état*], is already a State [*est déjà Etat*] . . ."[77] "And the political order? . . . The marvelous transcendence of the citizen, the great hope of the Enlightenment. To be sure, 'I was obscure in the other, but I was sovereign,' subject but prince. . . . The sovereignty shared as an equal is nonetheless the power-possibility of stoning free men, a criminal hostility toward the singular."[78] But it takes us as well to the conclusion of *La Grande Peur des bien-pensants* and its evocation of totalitarian discipline: "There can be no doubt that in feverishly completing the construction of the universal factory, the total Factory, millions upon millions of men naively believed they were fulfilling the oldest dream of French rationalism. On the pediment of that Temple of polytechnical science, the American entrepreneur would willingly inscribe, for your pleasure, the names of Rabelais, Voltaire, and Monsieur Anatole France."[79] Whereupon a call to resist the totalitarian course of history is issued to the youth of France ("jeunes gens français"): "As your revolutionary ancestors, incorrigible idealists, formerly proclaimed: 'Liberty or death,' a unanimous universe exhorts us today: 'Our discipline or death,' and believes it is saying exactly the same thing."[80] This is precisely Glucksmann's move in conflating the motifs of Rabelais's utopia (*Fay ce que voudras*) and Hitler's concentration camp (*Arbeit macht frei*) under the sinister umbrella of the Revolution. Bernanos ends his 1931 volume, moreover, with what is virtually an anticipation of a gas chamber: "We lack air [*l'air manque*]. The World that observes us with growing distrust is astonished to read in our eyes the same obscure anxiety. Already a few of us have stopped smiling, measure the obstacle at sight. . . . We won't be taken. . . . We won't be taken alive [*on ne nous aura pas vivants*]!"[81]

It is perhaps worth pausing to recall the elements of our homology between the configurations in Glucksmann (with Foucault) and in the Bernanos text of 1931: the Statist-Revolution as the vehicle of a generalized regime of surveillance (*panopticon, conciergerat*), culminating in a more or less cheery concentration camp which itself realizes, in sinister form, the ideals of the Enlightenment. A final—and decisive— item might be the odd appeal to a variety of priest that Glucksmann includes in the most personal part of his book ("Pourquoi ce long détour?"). Bernanos (quoting Drumont): "It is in our humblest priests that I place my hope. . . . Whatever happens, I am counting on one of those simple-hearted priests . . ."[82] Glucksmann: "In the light of history a life is barely any time. I have nevertheless on several occasions had the opportunity of seeing the majority of Frenchmen behave like scoundrels [*salauds*] . . . . In the resistance to the Nazi occupation, as in the resistance to the colonial war in Algeria, its massacres and tortures, priests came to occupy a decisive place, often in spite of their hierarchy or squarely in opposition to it. I respect them because I envy their courage . . . and generally because without them the air would be unbreathable in France. . . . May 68 was the opportunity for courageous priests . . ."[83] The appeal, then, to the antistatist priest, the insignia through which Glucksmann would perhaps cosign with Maurice Clavel, is part of an oblique but protracted homage to Bernanos.[84] Such would be the path from *La Grande Peur des bien-pensants* to "*La Grande Colère des faits.*"

Whereupon the strangeness of the filiation becomes all but manifest. For in relation to the panoptical monolith, Foucault-Glucksmann posits four exemplary renegades, of which the first is "the *Jew*, because he represents the absence of land, money that circulates, vagabondage, private interest, the immediate bond with God, as many ways of eluding the State. Anti-Semitism, which was fundamental in German thought of the nineteenth century, functioned as a protracted apology of the State. It was also the matrix of all the racisms branding madmen, deviants, aliens [*les métèques*] . . ."[85] Consider now that in *La Grande Peur*, the quintessential move whereby an individual, hopelessly, rises in insurrection against the monolith is the act wherein Edouard Drumont conceives and writes his philosophy of anti-Semitism. For that decision is seen by Bernanos as a declaration/demonstration of incompatibility with modern, statist, post-Revolutionary France: *la France juive*. In brief, we are presented with a chiasmus. Whereas Bernanos dreams the anti-Semite abandoning Jewish France, Glucksmann (with Foucault) has the Jew deserting an entity structurally identical, though it is taken to be fundamentally anti-Semitic. It is as odd a fate for French anti-Semitism as may be imagined. But then Bernanos had written: "If the work of Edouard Drumont today risks being misconstrued, it is because what is too often sought is a specific teaching, a positive doctrine, instead of attempting to see it in its entirety and, so to speak, in the rhythm and pulse of the anxiety out of which it was born, as a tragic experience, the sum total of the disappointments of a French heart [*la somme des déceptions d'un coeur français*]."[86] And if that rhythm were currently captured in France's anti-Marxian philosemitism?[87]

And Blanchot? His final text for *Combat*, "On demande des dissidents" (December 1937), is a protracted meditation on the transition "from the same to the same [*du même au même*]," the near impossibility of achieving the measure of heterogeneity termed dissidence.[88] "Comment la littérature est-elle possible?," the early pamphlet on Paulhan, focuses on "the nature of mind, its profound division, the combat of the Same with the Same [*ce combat du Même avec le Même*]."[89] The transition from Blanchot's political concerns to his thought on literature is situated between those texts, in the division separating their sameness. Historically, it is contemporaneous with the chiasmic reversal in the paradigm through which anti-Semite and Jew retained their relation. (Céline's *Bagatelles pour un massacre*, it should be recalled, meditated in 1937 a European holocaust organized *by* the Jews.) Blanchot (*La Folie du jour*): "Behind their backs, I detected the silhouette of the law. Not the law that is known, which is rigorous and scarcely agreeable: this one was different. Far from falling within the purview of its threat, it was I who seemed to frighten it. To believe its version, my gaze was thunder and my hands occasions to perish. In addition, it attributed to me, ludicrously, every power, perpetually declared itself at my knees. But it did not allow me to ask anything, and when it had granted me the right to be in all places, it meant that there was nowhere for me. When it placed me above the authorities, it meant: you are not authorized to do anything. If it humiliated itself: you don't respect me."[90]

V

In *L'Amitié*, Blanchot returned to the work of Jean Paulhan. In oblique summary of our argument, these three passages from that essay:

> I believe that the first letter I received from Jean Paulhan was dated 10 May 1940: "We shall long remember these days."[91]

> But is not that secret precisely the "fact" of reversal from for to against, of which Pascal, before Hegel, spoke to us and in a sense was wrong to speak to us, if it be true that such an operation can take effect only on the condition of not being proposed in a formulation that can retain it only at the cost of its liquidation.[92]

> As if, then, the ordeal through which the sense of that displacement—or, rather than its sense, its reality as event—were revealed implied its non-accomplishment, or as if we became aware of the leap [*saut*] only when, through our illicit discovery, we prevented it from coming to be, and, aggravating it in such wise, granted it its proper bearing, which would be to coincide with the eventuality of a death.[93]

II.

THE SUTURE OF AN ALLUSION: LACAN WITH LÉON BLOY

Toward the end of the first volume of his seminars to be published, *Les Quatre Concepts fondamentaux de la psychanalyse*, at the "foundation," then, of his "return to Freud," Jacques Lacan offers a surprisingly—egregiously—inappropriate allusion to the book that Léon Bloy regarded as the "most considerable" of his works, *Le Salut par les juifs*. Lacan: "Did I then present Freud to you last time in the figure of Abraham, Isaac, and Jacob? Léon Bloy, in *Le Salut par les juifs*, embodies them in the form of three equally old men who are there, according to one of the forms of Israel's vocation, indulging, around one can only imagine what stretch of canvas, in that fundamental occupation, the secondhand dealing called *la brocante*. They sort things out [*Ils trient*]. There's one thing they put on one side and another on the other. Freud puts partial drives [*les pulsions partielles*] on one side and love [*l'amour*] on the other. He says: *they're not the same* [*C'est pas pareil*]."[1] *C'est pas pareil*: one would expect, then, for the analogy to hold, that Bloy would evoke the discriminatory talent of the Jewish tinkerer or merchant, sorting out items even as Freud would distinguish between partial impulses or drives and a genital "love" subordinated to the needs—and delusions—of the ego. Indeed, given the simplicity (or flatness) of the comparison, one might even imagine Lacan less attracted by the image than by the title of the book—*Le Salut par les juifs*—insofar as it epitomized the program of psychoanalysis in its early phase. Freud, it will be recalled, observed, with misgiving, in a letter to Abraham, that psychoanalysis was becoming "a Jewish national affair . . ."[2] Whence a call for indulgence toward the Swiss . . .

Yet no sooner does one glance at the passage in Bloy to which Lacan

23

alludes, than one realizes the enormity of the psychoanalyst's—apparent—error. For Bloy's purpose is to recount the degree of moral and physical abjection to which humanity has descended in the figure of the Jew: "the contemporary Kike [*le Youtre moderne*] appears to be the confluence of every form of hideousness in the world" (p. 29).[3] He evokes the Jewish market in Hamburg, the almost physical malaise that he felt at the obsequiousness of the merchants, the "gelatinous flagellation" to which he felt exposed (p. 31). The arch-Jews, however, who bring Bloy to the brink of nausea, perhaps fainting, are three aged merchants, whom he imagines as Abraham, Isaac, and Jacob: "I will long remember, nevertheless, those three incomparable wretches [*crapules*] that I still see in their rotting smocks, leaning forehead to forehead over the orifice of a fetid sack that would have frightened the stars and in which were heaped up, for the exportation of typhus, the unspeakable objects of some arch-Semitic transaction" (p. 40). And it is to these Jews that Lacan compares Freud. To which the reader, above and beyond his or her distaste, perhaps shock, at the anti-Semitic tenor of the passage, can only respond, in the italicized words of Lacan's text: *c'est pas pareil*. As though the psychoanalyst, in that phrase, were unwittingly denouncing his own error. For the passage in Bloy is by no means an occasion for the exercise of discrimination, but rather a recollection of an encounter—in Hamburg—that brought the writer to the verge of fainting with disgust.

That the error should involve the question of anti-Semitism cannot but be of central interest for an understanding of the return to Freud; for psychoanalysis, it has been suggested, even as it puzzled out the possibility of a new economy of communication between unconscious and conscious modes of thought, remained a meditation on the difficulties of communication between Jews and the dominant Gentile society.[4] An abiding dilemma for Freud found its emblem in the query: on what terms does the Semite enter Rome, as the conquering avenger Hannibal, or as the converted aesthete Winckelmann; and the dreams of *Die Traumdeutung* are as obsessed with the near impossibility of promotion—to Professor *extraordinarius*—in anti-Semitic Vienna as with sexuality.[5] So that a confusion on the question of Jews and those repelled by them is a slip on a central issue.[6]

A blunder so gross on a subject so crucial by a reader as finely attuned to the nuances of Freud's text, it will be agreed, calls for interpretation. And it is to the strange logic—or aptness—of Lacan's inappropriate allusion to Bloy that I would like now to turn. To anticipate the direction of that interpretation, I would suggest that it turns on a *third* reading of the italicized phrase *c'est-pas-pareil*: no longer as a discrimination between *l'amour* and *les pulsions partielles* (Lacan's explicit sense); nor as a denunciation of the essential difference vitiating any assimilation of Freud-as-Jew to Bloy's merchants of Hamburg in the context of a "return to Freud"; but rather as a denial (*Verneinung*), in the psychoanalytic sense of the term, of the essential links between Lacan's text and Léon Bloy's *Le Salut par les juifs*. As though it were the Lacan-Bloy connection, in the *Séminaires*, that were suddenly being cut short by the assertion *c'est pas pareil*.[7]

Consider, first of all, the discursive position of Bloy in his text. *Le Salut par les juifs* is polemically directed against the degeneration of a tradition into that which that tradition was predicated against by dint of a failure to take into account its origins in a practice of textual interpretation. That tradition is quite simply (or complexly) the Christian medieval heritage of Jew-hating. In Bloy's words: "the Jews are, in sum, the most faithful witnesses, the most authentic curators of those candid Middle Ages which detested them *for the love of God* and which so often sought to exterminate them" (p. 80). Already it may be intuited that the unassimilable abjection of the Jews, their fidelity to that (faithless) abjection, will play so large a role in the economy of Christian experience as to constitute the irreducible medium within which the Christian drama will be played out. Such is the path that will bring Bloy to "salvation coming from the Jews (*Salus ex Judaeis est*)," the motif from chapter 4 of Saint John with which he entitles his book. But at this juncture I would insist rather that the onus of Bloy's fury is that the medieval tradition of Jew-hating, grounded in the exegesis of Scripture, had been liquidated in favor of what with Edouard Drumont and *La France juive* had become—by 1892—the big business of left-wing anti-Semitism.[8] Rooted as it was in the insipidly "middle-class" claim that the Jews had stolen the money of France and must be forced to return it, having debased the "Jewish question" "to the cerebral level of the most imbecilic members of the bourgeoisie," contemporary anti-Semitism had lost all contact with the cult of Poverty and the series of (sacred) texts in which it is sustained (p. 27). Whence Bloy's polemic.

Perhaps a snatch of Bloy's prose, "its style," as Bernanos put it, "of Byzantine opulence," may be of help here.[9] An English translation follows.

Quelques profanes, il est vrai, se sont demandé quelle victoire essentielle résidait, pour la morale — même *pratique* — dans l'indéniable fait d'avoir entrepris de substituer au fameux Veau d'or un cochon du même métal, et quel avantage précieux le Catholicisme allait retirer de ces récriminations d'agio.

Car enfin, M. Drumont entrait en héros dans Babylone, après avoir déconfit toutes les nations sémitiques, et les admirateurs de ce conquérant reniflaient sur lui la poussière du saint roi Midas, mêlée aux onguents et cinnamones dont s'adonise coutumièrement la carcasse des dieux mortels.

Pour parler moins lyriquement, ça marchait ferme, les gros tirages se multipliaient et les droits d'auteur s'encaissaient avec une précision rothschildienne qui faisait baver de concupiscence toute une jalouse populace d'écrituriers du même acabit qui n'avaient pas eu cette plantureuse idée et qui résolurent aussitôt de s'acharner aux mêmes exploits.

Tous les livides mangeurs d'oignons de la Haute et Basse Egypte comprirent admirablement que la guerre aux Juifs pouvait être, — à la fin des fins, — un excellent truc pour cicatriser maint désastre ou ravigoter maint négoce valétudinaire. (p. 23)

Some of the profane, it is true, wondered what essential victory resided for — even *practical* — morality in the undeniable fact of having undertaken to substitute for the famous Calf of Gold a pig of the same metal, and what precious advantage Catholicism would derive from those speculations in recrimination.

For Monsieur Drumont entered as a hero into Babylon after having discomfited all the Semitic nations, and the admirers of that conqueror sniffed on his person the dust of holy King Midas combined with the ointments and cinnamons with which the carcass of mortal gods is customarily adorned.

To speak less lyrically, business was going well, huge re-editions proliferated, and royalities were collected with a Rothschildlike precision which caused an entire jealous rabble of scribblers — who had not had that fertile idea and resolved forthwith to devote themselves unreservedly to identical expoits — to drool with cupidity.

All the livid consumers of the onions of Upper and Lower Egypt understood admirably that war on the Jews, in the last analysis, could be an excellent gimmick for patching up many a disaster and reinvigorating many an ailing business enterprise.

The impetus of the passage, then, is against the unscrupulous commercialization of Jew-hating in Drumont's anti-Semitic writings (and organizations). But it is on the specificity of the prose that I would insist: the short paragraphs, each a baroque sentence in length, that seem to end in relief that their violent extremes—Latinisms and *argot*, mythological allusions and the brand of facetiousness the French call *gouaille*—have nevertheless been contained by the proliferating syntax before their accumulated pressure can bring the page to the point of devastation. Those idiosyncrasies, and the seigneurial condescension in which they are couched, are closer to the distinctive features of Lacan's prose, I would suggest, than are those of any other French writer of the century.[10] Later in *Le Salut*, Bloy, quoting himself, wonders whether "some fanatic of my prose" would on some future occasion have recourse to the passage quoted (p. 48). Bloy's argumentative prose, then, like Lacan's, is of a variety intended to inspire in its violence extremes of fidelity above and beyond the content of its argument. Whence our interest in returning to the previously mentioned structure of that argument: a polemic directed against the degeneration of a tradition into that which it was originally predicated against, through a forgetting of its origin in a practice of textual exegesis or interpretation. For that evocation of Bloy's stance in *Le Salut par les juifs* captures as well the specificity of Lacan's "return to Freud": for failure to read, seriously, the grounding texts of Freud, the heart of psychoanalysis, the theory of repression, has itself been unwittingly repressed.[11] Whence the onslaught against "ego psychology" and the "American way of life" as the dismally profitable liquidation of all that is subversive in psychoanalysis.[12] Thus may we move, in our investigation of the motivation behind Lacan's inapt allusion to Bloy, from the phenomenology of style to considerations of argumentative structure and discursive position. Within each of the divergent traditions—psychoanalysis, Jew-hating—each would pretend to restore to its originary energy, Lacan and Bloy would appear to fulfill homologous roles.

For the author of *Le Salut par les juifs*, the world is less a text than two discrete series whose recurrent failure to coincide with each other marks the repetitive rhythm (out) of history itself. There is ideally an end to History when the recurring events of the Old Testament are finally absorbed or fulfilled *figurally* by those of the New. What interests Bloy, however, is the energy—of Judaism—spent in maintaining the difference of that double inscription, preventing History from being fulfilled, affirming "the *impossible* betrothal [*accordailles*] of the two Testaments" (p. 150).[13] For separating both series, setting history itself askew, is the circularity of the following paradox: "The

Jews will convert only when Jesus will have descended from his Cross, and Jesus, precisely, can descend from it only when the Jews will have converted" (p. 122). That circularity figures a double bind retarding the movement of history in an essential way, opening it to a horrendous synchrony, the cruel parody of that end of Time attendant on the fulfillment of Figures: "The history of the Jews obstructs [*barre*] the history of the human race as a dike obstructs a river. . . . They are forever unmoving" (pp. 44-45).[14]

Turn now to Lacan and the motif of the detained *lettre en souffrance*, which his seminar on Poe posits as the specialty of psychoanalysis. For the focus of Bloy's essay is the crucifying pain through which the Jew holds up delivery of the letter of the "préfigurant" to its destination in the "préfiguré" (p. 66).[15] Indeed the specificity of *Le Salut par les juifs* is its will to think the error of Judaism in its irreducible positivity, beyond any reduction to—or through—the category of illusion. Bloy would *affirm* the heterogeneity of the Jews in the very element of their unthinkable and unredeemable difference.[16] And it is that refusal to *absorb* the Jews into any philosophical or theological synthesis which again brings us to Lacan. For "the Jewish question" had received an eminently "synthetic" treatment several years prior to Lacan's seminar by Sartre.[17] The Jew, for Sartre, derived the whole of his continued existence from the hatred of the anti-Semite. The Jew's deluded synthesis, fundamentally suicidal, was thought rife with all the illusions and aggressions of what Freud termed narcissism and Lacan analyzed in terms of the *mirror stage*. Sartre, pursuing his thematic of a dialectic *pour autrui*, would resolve the Jewish question through a rectified "application" of the "synthetic spirit."[18] For he shares with anti-Semite and Jew a sense of the urgency of a synthetic formulation, and is opposed with them to the atomizing "analytic spirit" of the "democrat."[19] Whereupon a third position, which Lacan encounters in Bloy: "a synthesis of the Jewish question is absurdity itself, outside of the prior acceptance of the prejudice of an *essential excision* [*un retranchement essentiel*], a sequestration of Jacob in the most abject decrepitude" (p. 41). Moreover, that primal unassimilability has its locus in the circle of pain that maintains the two textual series, beyond teleology, discrete, retaining the letter of the Old Testament *en souffrance*. Whence the interest of observing that Lacan, in the seminar just prior to that alluding to Bloy, insists on the drive *missing* its object, having its aim in the circular trajectory that is its essence: "that form which the drive may take of attaining its satisfaction without attaining its aim . . . it is a partial drive [*pulsion partielle*] and . . . its aim is nothing but this circuitous return" (p. 163).[20] In brief, and (necessarily) schematically, the three positions on "the Jewish question" I have alluded to reproduce the three instances of the structure of Lacan's *Séminaire sur 'la Lettre volée'*, that is, of psychoanalysis itself:[21]

1. What Sartre calls the analytic atomism of the democrat corresponds to the "realism" of the ego psychologist. In French, the ego psychologist who has pondered "the Jewish question" most extensively is R. Loewenstein in his *Psychanalyse de l'antisémitisme*.[22]

2. Sartre's own analysis of Judaism and its mirror-image anti-Semitism in terms of a dialectic of false consciousness [*pour autrui*] reproduces the general configuration of deluded subjectivity — as opposed to the deluded "objectivity" of 1 — thematized in psychoanalysis in terms of narcissism.

3. Bloy's affirmation of the Jew in terms of the pulsating irreducibility of two parallel textual series and the letters inhibited from arriving at their prefigured destination brings us finally to the position of the unconscious. It is at this level that the concept of repetition functions at its most radical and seems less inherited by Lacan from the synchrony of the structuralists than from the tortured speculations of Bloy. Lacan: "it is through repetition, as the repetition of unfulfillment [*déception*], that Freud coordinates experience, as essentially unfulfilling, with a reality [*réel*] that will henceforth be situated, in the domain of science, as what the subject is condemned to miss [*manquer*], but which that very failure [*manquement*] reveals."[23] The passage seems as much a comment on Bloy's Jews as on desire itself.

* * *

In part 3 of *Moses and Monotheism*, Freud suggested that one of the grounds for anti-Semitism was the "grudge" that the Christians held against the Mosaic code they had inherited with its concomitant imperative of "instinctual — or better: drive — renunciation (*Triebverzicht*)."[24] Freud's dismantling of the fierce Mosaic heritage, begun already in the *immobilizing* analysis of the *Moses* of Michelangelo, has thus been available to interpretation in terms of a desire to loosen the affective hold of the vast anti-Jewish machine which was soon to dominate

Europe and had already pursued Freud himself out of Vienna.[25] To that extent, it has been suggested, psychoanalysis itself might be figured as part of the historic effort to free Judaism from the burden of the Mosaic code and its vengeful God. Now one encounters an oddly similar development in *Le Salut par les juifs*. Under the rubric "The First Jewish Speculation," Bloy sees Abraham, bargaining with God for the "amnesty of Sodom" (*Genesis*, 18), as the first Jewish businessman: Will you save the city for the sake of fifty, no, forty-five, what about forty, etc., honest men?[26] On the one hand, Sodom and Gommorah, with their currency: *les pulsions partielles*; on the other: *l'amour . . . de Dieu*—the two items sorted out by Lacan's *brocanteur* in the allusion to Bloy. And indeed, the elaborate symbolic transaction through which Sodom and Gommorah might gain some *droit de cité* is perhaps not a bad emblem for the therapeutic project of psychoanalysis. But Bloy, in fact, does not use the word *brocanteur* to describe Abraham, but rather to characterize that other Jewish merchant, *prefigured*, he writes, by Abraham in negotiating Sodom's fate: Judas Iscariot, "peddler [*brocanteur*] of God," arranging "the sale of Christ" (pp. 75, 161). Which is to suggest that the apparently liberatory Jewish gesture of psychoanalysis, in this reading, was always already governed by its repetition *après coup* as the Biblical sequence most available as a justification for oppression (of the Jews).[27] As though the allusion to Bloy were Lacan's return to—or devastating assumption of—the testament Freud had left in *Moses and Monotheism*.

An interpretation? Riffaterre, in a recent article, invokes the Piercean notion of interpretant as a mediator between text and intertext. (Thus Mallarmé is the *interpretant* of Derrida's reading of Hegel at the beginnning of *Glas*.)[28] In this sense, Bloy would serve as an interpretant, in my reading, of Lacan's reading of Freud. Yet the conflictual core of the present interpretation seems better captured by the Freudian notion of "family romance": the fantasy of a noble parent to replace a humble one.[29] As though the return to Freud—to whom history has granted the nobility of Jewish genius—in fact masked an unwitting return to the—unreadable—Léon Bloy of *Le Salut par les juifs*.[30] It is a schema whose irony may be fully gauged only upon consideration of Freud's own family romance as acted out in *Moses and Monotheism* and a host of shorter texts. To these we now shall turn.

THE SUTURE OF AN ALLUSION

* * *

Several years before Léon Bloy's transfixing encounter with the Jewish merchants of Hamburg, Sigmund Freud, in the summer of 1882, traveled to Hamburg and underwent a memorable encounter with a Jewish merchant in the ghetto of that city. It is discussed in an extended letter to his *fiancée*, Martha Bernays, of 23 July 1882.[31] The tradesman sold Freud the monogrammed paper on which he wrote the letter evoking their meeting. In fact, however, that paper, monogrammed with the "entwined" [*innig verschlungen*] characters *S* and *M*—for Sigmund and Martha—was intended, writes the jealous Freud, for letters that Martha could address—because of the monogram—to him alone. At stake, then, in the encounter with the Hamburg merchant, were the conditions allowing Freud to inscribe his desire (as the desire of an other), surely a matter of fundamental concern to a historian of psychoanalysis. Some forty years later, in *Beyond the Pleasure Principle*, Freud would press his formulations to an extreme in his speculations about the "speculative" play of his grandson Ernst unreeling a toy spool away from himself and then retrieving it to the rhythm of *Fort-Da*.[32] Freud, on the path to the death instinct, evokes that scene and ascribes it to a *Bemächtigungstrieb*, an "instinct to master." Perhaps that development is already present in the letter to Martha, or rather in the sheets of paper, monogrammed *S* and *M*, he sent her in order better to assure their "return to Freud." (And indeed, Freud's 1920 speculations on grandson Ernst's game of *Fort-Da*, read in conjunction with Ernst's edition, some years later, of grandfather Sigmund's epistolary version of *Fort-Da*, offers as fine an emblem of the circularity of the drive [Lacan] as might be wished.) As though the encounter with the Hamburg merchant were already inciting Freud to move beyond the pleasure principle.

More explicitly, the encounter helped him move, he writes in the letter, beyond another reality—a certain relation to Judaism. For Freud's ill-kempt Jew ("his beard was shaggy, *struppig*"), like many a Jew of Hamburg, and no doubt like the three whom Lacan borrows from Bloy, derived his sense of Judaism from a single man, the *chacham* of Hamburg, Isaac Bernays, grandfather of Martha: "we owe our education to a single man . . ." The idiosyncratic content of Bernays's teaching, as summarized by the merchant, is the Jewish imperative to enjoyment, the scorn for those incapable of pleasure [*Er verachtete jeden der nicht geniessen könne . . .*]. The relation to what would later emerge as psychoanalysis may be intuited.[33] Freud, in a curious sentence, speaks of the inadequacy of reform to sustain that tradition, the necessity of a revolution [*Umsturz*] that would nevertheless appear to remain *within* Judaism. Thus did Freud embark on the path that would eventually take him to a discussion of "The Truth in Religion," the psychical reality informing the delusions of Judaism, toward the end of *Moses and Monotheism*.[34]

Freud's letter is introduced by an epigraph from *Nathan der Weise*.[35] For Freud imagines the merchant as the wily hero of Lessing's play. In that play, a Jewish daughter is made to suffer at the thought that her beloved Jewish father, Nathan, had in fact adopted her. The instrument of that pain is the Christian knight templar who has fallen in love with her. Recha (the daughter): "*Giebt nimmer zu, dass mir / Ein andrer Vater aufgedrungen werde . . .*" [Never allow a different father to be pressed upon me . . .]. These are perhaps the pained words with which Freud, more than a half-century later, imagined the Jews receiving his *Moses and Monotheism*, the presumably traumatic revelation that Moses was, in fact, an Egyptian nobleman who had "stooped" to tell the Jews they were his children.[36] The verb *stoop* communicates strangely with Freud's recollection, in *Die Traumdeutung*, of his humiliated father stooping in the gutter to retreive his hat after it had been knocked off his head by an anti-Semite.[37] It would appear, then, that in *Moses and Monotheism* Freud's "revolution" at some level constituted an acting out of his family romance: the replacement of a shameful Jewish father by a noble Gentile one.[38] It is worth noting, then, that in the parallel with Lessing's play, if the merchant of Hamburg, disciple of Bernays, recalls to Freud Nathan, Freud himself, in love with Bernays's granddaughter, finds himself— unwittingly—in the role of the medieval knight templar, repelled (initially) at the very idea of confronting a Jew: "er kömmt zu keinem Juden . . ." The Jew(ess) deprived of her Jewish father; Freud as the Gentile crusader (giving tours of Mount Sinai!): the motifs that bring Freud to evoke Lessing's play in his discussion of the Jewish merchant of Hamburg offer some indication of the extent to which the family romance that would be acted out in what Freud was originally inclined to call his "historical novel" on Moses was already latent in the letter of 23 July 1882.[39] But the figure of medieval Christian repelled at the prospect of encountering the Jewish merchant of Hamburg reproduces precisely the configuration in Bloy that Lacan, inexplicably, had alluded to. A double family romance, then. On the one hand, Freud, just prior to World War II, dreaming the Jews children of a noble Gentile; on the other, Lacan, after the war, celebrating his descendance from the Jew Freud in a "return to Freud" intent on obliterating all trace of a "return to Bloy."[40] The figure of that repetition is chiasmus. Or, in Lacan's terms, the return to Freud might best be read in terms of that formula for intersubjective communication on which the Seminar on "The Purloined Letter" ends and which has oriented these remarks—"in which the sender, we tell you, receives from the receiver his own message in inverse form."[41]

III.

A FUTURE FOR *ANDROMAQUE:*
ARYAN AND JEW
IN GIRAUDOUX'S FRANCE

> Quelle leçon donner à l'Europe, si c'est
> justement un Français, de ce peuple agité,
> qui décide de prendre racine et de porter
> des bourgeons et des feuilles!
>
> —Giraudoux, *Portugal* (1941)

Literature, it has been suggested, may best be defined, given the habits of the age, with minimal transcendence, as the texts read for courses so labeled in the universities. The institutional reality of the subject "French literature" takes on a curious configuration in this light. For departments of French literature, for better or for worse, have proved such effective hosts for that generalized *para*philosophical, *para*psychoanalytic meditation on interpretation termed "poststructuralism" that it appears at times as though the host organisms were themselves sustained by—the enthusiasms generated by—their parasite. "French literature," that is, would seem, to paraphrase Freud, no longer to be master in its own (academic) house—a residue, however, whose very marginality may merit new attention. And it is to "French literature" as an institution, an actualized intersection of fantasy and belief, that these pages are devoted, more specifically to a writer, Giraudoux, whose virtuosity seems so completely in the service of an ideal or ideology of French literature that one suspects that the current relative lack of interest in the considerable pleasures of his text is in large measure understandable as a reaction against that institution.

Littérature française was, in fact, the original title of the volume of essays Giraudoux was to collect and publish in 1941 as *Littérature*: a would-be renewal of a crucial national resource in a tragic time. In

a defeated and occupied France, literature would engage history as
virulent, performative [*agissant*], and, beyond any academic domes-
tication, more passionately historical than the sham that the French
had come to take for history itself: "our true history . . . and sole
source of retribution" (p. 18).[1] On 31 January 1944, several months
prior to the Liberation of Paris, Giraudoux died suddenly of an attack
of uremia. Aragon would report that he had been poisoned by the Gestapo.[2] Céline dashed off a note of outrage at the rallying of patriotic
sentiment around the event of the playwright's death and had it published 11 February in *Je suis partout*: "On the side, the Jews must be
having a good laugh reading the Giraudoux obituaries . . . Everybody
understands . . . in the name of *belles-lettres* . . . the dignity of
French thought and so on! The shmucks [*Jean-foutres*]! . . . Every
day they make you sad to be an Aryan . . ."[3] In brief, the timing of
Giraudoux's death was such, midst the general confusion of imminent
liberation, as to free him for the public imagination as an exemplary
casualty of the war. Giraudoux had left behind *La Folle de Chaillot*,
and its first performance, 19 December 1945, a benefit for the Association des Résistants de 1940, with de Gaulle and Malraux attending,
was the theatrical event of the Liberation.[4] The militancy of *Littérature* (*française*), then, one of Giraudoux's final legacies to France,
would appear to be one of Resistance. And indeed the ethical and
political urgency with which "French literature" was (once) taught
in this country by a previous generation owed much, one suspects, to
an amorphous but unmistakable mystique of Resistance.[5]

Thus runs a myth of Giraudoux, virtuoso ideologue of French literature. My aim in what follows is less to demolish than to dismantle
it: beginning with *Littérature*, we will trace a network of relations—
or prolegomena—which converge in their intricacy on that artistic
culmination of the Liberation (in Paris), that classic of undergraduate
performance (in the United States), *La Folle de Chaillot*. The necessity of that convergence, however, will come to bear with a force so
opposed to the play's apparent thrust as to unsettle to some degree
the ideological construct "French literature" itself.

Littérature: Of the four exemplary figures to whom chapters are
devoted at the beginning of Giraudoux's volume, pride—and uniqueness—of place is accorded to Racine, "first writer of French letters"
(p. 21). This need hardly surprise even a casual reader of the plays.
The image of destiny in *La Guerre de Troie n'aura pas lieu* is, of course,

Andromaque widowed, Astyanax orphaned—the starting point of Racine's first important tragedy. An initial discordance, then, may already be perceived between the disastrous course of French history in the 1930s and what our author qualifies as "the intangible domain and true value of the French venture in the world" (p. 6). And indeed much of the reading of Giraudoux that follows may be regarded as an explication of that future for Racine—or *Andromaque*—which his work celebrates and performs.

The uniqueness of Racine's place in *Littérature* becomes apparent early in the essay on the book's second representative man, Laclos. For "his was the appearance, the last in our literature, the belated, impassive, glacial but undeniable appearance, of the only one never to adulterate, stutter, compromise, or blink: Racine" (p. 56). Racine and his delayed return in Laclos thus constitute something of a composite formation, which we shall treat as such, always attendant to a fundamental difference that marks their repetition. For Laclos offers an exacerbation of Racine: "He pressed to its extreme the Racinian theory by eliminating love from the amorous character, and replacing it with eroticism; he situated, that is, the true struggle between man and woman not in resistance, but in facility" (p. 63). Laclos is Racine *unbound*: his heroine and her consort "bring to their ultimate pitch and their true and irremediable limit all the passions to which the greatest plays gave only one-sided and middle-class conclusions" (p. 65). Now this repetition of the Racinian couple, its love expended to the point of intense, erotic indifference, has important resonances for the reader of Giraudoux's plays. For the general economy of the entirety of his theater finds its pivot in a crucial split *between couples*: Andromaque's ultimate sadness is less to lose Hector than to realize that history will have as its vehicle the perfectly indifferent "love" of Helen of Troy; Electre, incestuously bound to Oreste, denounces Clytemnestre, in the last analysis, for not even loving Egisthe. This genesis (through repetition) of what the Laclos essay calls "the marriage of evil . . . the perfect couple" and the text of its denunciation lie at the center of Giraudoux's theater. Such is the discovery that organizes Charles Mauron's remarkable superimposition of the plays: "the two women in the center, the pathetic figure accusing the other, in her objectivity, of lacking love . . . and lying . . ."[6] But the relevance of Mauron's book brings us to a strange juncture in the history of criticism in France as well. For *Le Théâtre de Giraudoux*, Mauron's final (posthumous) work of 1971, is in many ways a moving revision of his 1957 study of a different series of plays, *L'Inconscient dans l'oeuvre et la vie de Racine*.[7] The 1971 effort entailed a curious return to that of 1957: "starting with *La Guerre de Troie n'aura pas lieu* there occurs in Giraudoux's myth something recalling, in certain aspects, the schema of Racine: the aggressiveness changes direction—but the meaning of the shift is quite different. The splitting of the Edenic couple appears increasingly fated, and two images of the couple emerge."[8] The reference to Racine is inseparable from the duplication-degeneration of the couple. As in the essay on Laclos, whose novel Giraudoux terms both "belated [*retardataire*]" and "anticipatory [*précurseur*]" (p. 66) . . . Be it in the history of criticism (Mauron's *Racine* was to have an issue in Barthes's volume and all that ensued therefrom), in the structure of Giraudoux's theater, or in his fantasy of French literature and its historical mission, our inquiry returns to the legacy of Racine, the future to be accorded *Andromaque*.

An answer of sorts to that dilemma is offered at the end of the Racine-Laclos intertext. The expenditure of Racine in his latter-day repetition is tantamount to a curious vengeance, whose formula is: "Racine aided by Vauban . . . Whereupon Andromaque surrenders, Phèdre surprises Hippolyte in her bed, Roxane kills Bajazet, but after being sated, and Iphigénie, though she has nothing to do with any of it, is raped in passing. All the murders and suicides in Racine take place, but after consummation [*après jouissance*], and dissipated bodies only remain to be decapitated" (p. 66). Thus does Giraudoux, at the tail end of the chapter, modulate into another region of his theatrical mythology, leave Greece behind, and direct us to the murder after consummation of the only one of his plays he designated a "tragedy," *Judith*. Whereupon, after the fact, the entire Racine chapter takes on a certain readability. For *Judith* is a dismantling of the theological myth. At the crux of the play, the proud Jewess encounters Holophernes, "a man, at last, of this world," who seduces her into the Edenic clarity of his Godless existence, woos her away from the "exaltation of the Jews" with such consummate passion that her murder of him, between acts 2 and 3, figures as a "supreme form of tenderness," assurance that the perfection of their night together will know no decline (p. 278).[9] The Jewess has given her reading of the myth: "Between her people and Holophernes, she has chosen love" (p. 303). But the rest of the play consists of the ruses whereby the

Jews—and their God—recathect the myth, obliterate Judith's *meurtre-après-jouissance*, "embalm their lie in canticles" (p. 302). Enter Racine. For just as Judith constituted a—failed—effort to snatch a saving core of godlessness from the mythology of the Jews, "Racine" is a protracted attempt to cleanse the poet's brief career of all links with the religion of Port-Royal: "His crises, his religious yearnings? . . . He had with the Jansenists the disputes of a choirboy with the deacons. Pascal had them with God" (p. 24). Giraudoux begins an imagined epitaph for Racine: "Here lies he who never posed the question of God . . ." (p. 27). Jansenism, of course, is not Judaism, but at both extremes of Racine's career, the Jewish reference—or metaphor—surfaces. First: "His retreat into the sacred precincts did not make of him a levite, but a provincial . . ." (p. 25). And, finally, concerning the Biblical plays: "he at last found a fate more pitiless than that of antiquity, whose virulence had been tempered by the disbelief of the Greeks and the poetic horizon. He found his people. He can, with the Jews, trade in his Greek Destiny for a Jehovah who, in addition to the native cruelty of Zeus, has precise designs on humanity" (p. 36). But the "Judaism" that closes in on Racine at the end, after *Phèdre*, is of course also simultaneous with the "silence" of Racine. "His characteristic style itself had become alien to him; he forgot it: in *Athalie*, he uses whole hexameters from *Andromaque* or other plays, so little had he reread himself in the last ten years. Transformed into a callous man in a world become insensitive, it was not surprising that his reticence was absolute" (p. 44). Judith, undone by the Angel, knows a comparable silence. The Chief Rabbi, Joachim, instructs her just before the end of the play: "If the word love and word bliss [*jouissance*] are still in your mouth, shout them, if you like, a last time; spit them out toward us before the supreme silence" (p. 314). The word *jouissance*, in fact, recurs in the characterization of theater in "Racine": "The spectator demands of his spectacle only enjoyment [*jouissances*]" (p. 28). But no sooner is that extreme pleasure evoked than Giraudoux reverts to a metaphor of murder: "He is no more concerned with perfecting the instruments of theater than a killer is the dagger forged for him by honest cutlers. It's blood the killer is after, and the young Racine as well" (p. 28). *Meurtre-après-jouissance*, as the Laclos text ended. At the core of the "Racine" chapter, we find the fantasy—from *Judith*—that will close the entire Racine-Laclos intertext.

Let us posit, then, that *Judith* offers the schema that most fundamentally informs the sequence on which *Littérature* opens. The French
national tragedy would prompt Giraudoux to reintroduce "French literature" as *his* "tragedy." Yet consider that the noble Holophernes's
project, in 1931, was the extermination of the Jews. Otta, in act 2,
warns his master: "Beware, my lord, beware. Consider that from your
embrace with this maiden will be born a series of beings and symbols
already almost eradicated from the universe, designers of men's hats
and usury, virtuosos and prophesy" (p. 269). Genocide is the order of
the day, and one dimension of Giraudoux's tragedy is the obliteration
of Holophernes's project. The play tells of how the Jews snatched back
their myth from the French playwright in his ingenious effort to ex-
propriate it. With strange incongruity, Holophernes-Giraudoux reacti-
vates the structure of *Judith*, a play lamenting a failed genocide, as
consolation against the invasion of France by a power whose most
radical program for Europe was an extermination of the Jews.

An interpretation? The reinvention of the tradition, according to
Littérature, in the face of national disaster, was to find its model in
that sudden sense of consolation or revenge which many a reader has
experienced in relation to the events of his or her private existence.
Whence the case cited of the bureaucrat relieved of his frustrations by
the insight with which he discovered them formulated in the writings
of Montesquieu. Now it happens that the single outstanding failure of
Giraudoux's theatrical career was the harsh critical reception accorded
Judith in 1931.[10] Gide's reaction in his *Journal* was not uncharacter-
istic: "If we may well admit that Judith is taken with Holophernes,
one does not see at all well how she comes to kill him. 'Out of love,'
she affirms. But she really has to tell us for us to realize it . . . It is
hard to extricate the emotion of certain scenes from the brilliance and
iridescence with which an overly precious style adorns them."[11] More
generally, Giraudoux was condemned, as *Action française* put it, for
offering less a play than a literary exercise, and *Judith* was withdrawn
from the stage after forty-five performances. The author's personal
humiliation, then, was revived at the time of the national humiliation,
and the fantasy of "literature" redeeming both may have inflected the
composition of the opening chapters of *Littérature*. The situation is
complicated, however, by the existence of another *Judith*, Henry
Bernstein's play of 1922.[12] For Bernstein's play knew as profound a
success as Giraudoux's was to encounter failure. Colette, in 1922, had

written that *Judith* would make of Bernstein "a classic."[13] Claude Farrère, in *Le Gaulois*, did not hesitate to invoke *Athalie*.[14] And Antoine, in 1931, in a review of Giraudoux, was to declare his preference for *Judith* 1922.[15] Bernstein's play, its local color underwritten by snatches of Hebrew transliterated in the text, was perceived by its admirers in 1922 as a superlative exercise in Orientalism. Thus L. Dubech in *Action française*: *Judith* is "like an Oriental garden laden with cumbrous roses. In all ages, our Western souls have feared the seduction of intellectual exaltation midst those fragrances, harmonies, intoxicating splendors."[16] And P. Mille, in *La Renaissance*, defends the apparent "brutality" of the play by suggesting that the proper context for understanding Bernstein's work is the Bible read with the Orientalist studies of Gobineau.[17] Thus wrote *Judith*'s admirers in 1922. Here, twenty years later, is the substance of a diatribe *against* Bernstein: "the whole, couched in a dialogue that is a dejection of drunken adjectives vociferated by sonorous mannequins—a megaphone in their gut and the gesticulation of madmen in a total fit."[18] That characterization, however adequate it may appear to the incipient hysteria of *Judith*, is taken from Lucien Rebatet's infamous tract of 1941, in the series "Les Juifs en France," *Les Tribus du cinéma et du théâtre*. In it, Bernstein is said to be the single figure "who could epitomize by himself the whole of Jewish theater in France."[19] From 1922 to 1941, then, for its admirers as for its detractors, Bernstein's *Judith* was regarded as an essentially Jewish property. Whence the complex situation of Giraudoux's version. Its subject is the (failed) attempt to win Judith from the Jews. But *Judith* 1931 was, to all appearances, a (failed) effort to win the (subject of the) play—perhaps the theater itself—from the Jews. And it was the bitterness of that dual failure which Giraudoux imagined as implicitly cognate with the humiliation of France itself in 1941. This is an admittedly speculative reading, one whose roots and implications in the rest of Giraudoux's *oeuvre* remain to be gauged. But already at this juncture, and in partial confirmation, we may recall that in one of his earliest references to *Littérature*, Giraudoux told an interviewer from *Je suis partout* in April 1938 that the first of the authors he would study in his *Littérature française* would be neither Racine nor Laclos, but Gobineau.[20] Two weeks earlier, Rebatet had published his scurrilous special issue of the same journal on *Les Juifs* . . ."[21]

I

In his attempt to elaborate through a superimposition of Giraudoux's plays the structured conflict underwriting them, Mauron chose first to examine *Judith*, the only "tragedy," and its points of friction or unexpected repetition in relation to the novels that until 1930 had dominated his output. For it was with *Judith*, one senses, that theater was to assume its centrality in his work, and that he was to imagine himself as initiating in France a romanticism of the stage that Hugo, a hundred years earlier, had been able to do no better than bluff.[22] The transition to the stage, however, had been made three years earlier, in 1928, in the stage version of *Siegfried et le Limousin: Siegfried*. Both novel and play have been read—inadequately—as fanciful allegories of the essential France and Germany. In fact, as we shall see, most of the characters are—differently—Franco-German, and therein lies the drama. The fundamental situation in both works pits Zelten, on the eve of an abortive putsch, against the great man of the Weimar Republic, Siegried von Kleist. Siegfried had been discovered nude, wounded, in a state of total amnesia, on a battlefield during the war, and had risen—meteorically—to prominence thereafter. Zelten's trump is his knowledge that Siegfried is not German, but the French journalist Jacques Forestier, believed to be a casualty of the war. As the truth of his past closes in on him, moreover, Siegfried finds himself vacillating between two women, his—i.e., Forestier's—French *fiancée*, Geneviève, and his German protectress, Eva.[23] Finally Zelten, on the eve of exile (to Montparnasse) after the failure of his putsch, reveals Siegried's foreign birth. In the final version of the play, Siegfried-Forestier returns to France as well with the tentative hope of combining his two national experiences into a "logical tissue," of elaborating therefrom a "new science" (p. 84).[24]

In terms of the field of forces subtending the play, it is clear that if Zelten is opposed to Siegfried (and Eva), his political interest lies in the restoration of Forestier to his identity, the reconstitution of the couple Forestier-Geneviève. The full measure of that solidarity—which structures Giraudoux's myth—is, however, masked by the gradual obliteration of the political profiles of each of the characters as they are transformed from the novel of 1922 to the play six years later. To that process we now shall turn.

Zelten, whose character is most severely truncated in the 1928 version, is above all a German enamored of France. He bears the tatoo *The-German-possessing-this-skin-will never-hate-France* and—to that extent —the sympathies of the author as well (p. 33).[25] For Siegfried, the bastion of Weimar, is in the novel the creature of the *Antifranzosenhassliga.* Zelten's politics are antirepublican, anticapitalist, an exaltation of old German values. His day-long revolution, however, seems marked by a single concern: the Jews. In the novel, no sooner is the revolution declared than the narrator turns to a squadron of Russian Jews assembled in Munich, without for the while knowing whether they are to be the "quarry" or the "hunters" (p. 224). Two pages later we learn that all the Jews of Schwabing have been arrested. The Jew Lieviné-Lieven, his name yoking together in parody the names of two Spartacists, tells his wife cynically that Zelten will not last: "To whom does Germany belong, if not us? . . . Let Zelten find me a boat, a theater, a barge of which we are not masters. . . . The beak of the German eagle is our nose" (p. 229). Lieviné-Lieven will not appear in *Siegfried* 1928, and it is instructive to trace the disappearance of his imprint in the text. It begins already in 1922: "A corrosive, in his childhood, having rendered his palms undecipherable . . ." (p. 246). Now in a scene that was subsequently cut from the play, but published by Giraudoux in 1928 as "Divertissement de Siegfried," the same obliterated imprint recurs. The circumstance is the single act available for Zelten to perform before his abdication, the pardoning of a criminal. The criminal, a Galician Jew, enters and is described by an officer: "He must be a known bandit. Instead of donning gloves for his crimes, he burned away every surface of his hand and fingers that could leave prints."[26] We are, then, in direct communication with Lieviné-Lieven here. Now it happens that the Galician Jew is of the last surviving family of the town of Slop, believed by philologists to have been destroyed thirty years earlier. The news astonishes Robineau, Zelten's French friend, who relates his elation: "But Slop, Zelten, is that city which all the universities of the world believe extinct; it is the birthplace of poetic Yiddish—the only place it was pure, graceful, sensuous. It is the Yiddish City of Ys. All Yiddish love songs come from Slop. For ten years I've been searching in books and in tradition for what I find in this man now. He has the keys to my career."[27] Robineau pleads with Zelten to pardon the criminal, but to no avail. The Jew, moreover, in the course of his plea, reveals himself capable of every baseness, including the prostitution of his daughter. Zelten's only accomplishment in his one-day revolution has been in consummating a small genocide of the Jews. He abdicates his dictatorship proudly, revealing the basis for his defeat in two intercepted telegrams: one from the United States, cutting off Germany's oil supply, the other a threat on Germany's currency from London. But his final insult consists in casting Siegfried with the Jews of Weimar: "On the heels of what amnesia your friends Rathenau, Harden, and Schneidemann infiltrated into Germany it is not for me to say, nor the complaints in Yiddish they whined when they were little. . . . Adieu, messieurs" (p. 256). Zelten's *coup*, in the 1922 novel, took place in Munich. The 1928 play, however, is set in Gotha. In between came Hitler's failed putsch of 1923. In light of which, one is hard put to interpret the shift of locale in other terms than those of an attempt to deny a barely avoidable assimilation of Zelten with Hitler.

The crucial element in Zelten's revolution was the defeat of Weimar through the restoration of Forestier (Siegfried) to his brutally interrupted past. Now concerning that past, perhaps the most remarkable clue given us in the novel refers to a ceremony commemorating Forestier's alleged death: "There were present, without their personnel, the editors of the nationalist and monarchist newspapers, since Forestier belonged, in the afternoon, to the *Revue critique*, and, without the editors, the petty personnel of the extreme left-wing newspapers on which Forestier collaborated in the evening to earn a living, *Lanterne* or *Progrès civique*" (p. 15). This curious combination of extreme Left and Right recurs toward the end of act 1 of the play, in which Geneviève recalls to Siegfried the habits that bound her to her *fiancé* during the two years of their love, from 1912 to 1914: "At six o'clock, you returned to the *Action française*, where you wrote a royalist article on the Chambre, and I went to pick you up at eight at the *Lanterne*, where you were finishing off the socialist article on the Senate. And that was two years of our life, Jacques" (p. 29). Now these details are among those allowing intimates of Giraudoux to identify Forestier as a version of Giraudoux's friend, André du Fresnois, who disappeared during the war. The novelist, indeed, would later report that it was du Fresnois's death that had given him the idea for his book.[28] Now du Fresnois represented for many of his contemporaries nothing less than the future of criticism. Paul Morand speaks of him as "destined to be the most brilliant critic of his generation."[29] And André Billy waxed particularly eloquent to the same effect: "If the Germans, in killing Alain-Fournier, did irremediable damage to our literature, and in particular to the novel, the injury sustained by French criticism was no less in the case of the disappearance of André du Fresnois. . . . When we used to speak of those who already formed the literary elite of our generation, André du Fresnois customarily said: 'First there is Jean Giraudoux.' . . . *Lectures pour une ombre* by Giraudoux is dedicated to 'André du Fresnois, missing [*disparu*].' It is, in fact, only to a minimal error of modern ballistics that the survivor, J. G., owes it to be still breathing the air in which are scattered, afloat, the remains of du Fresnois."[30] The link between Giraudoux and the fallen du Fresnois appears to have been so intense that J. Body, the most accomplished of Giraudoux scholars, refers to it as a "personal myth" of the author: "according to which his friend, brother or double, fallen in the war, fell for him and was reborn in—or for—him."[31] The term *personal myth*, with its barrage of psychoanalytic resonances, perhaps finds its justification in Giraudoux's sense of the specificity of French theater itself: "The impression sustained by a Frenchman faced with a tragedy, anxiety, or emotion, comes to him not from seeing his fate acted out on stage by superior powers, but from the remorse and gratitude he experiences at feeling his tranquillity on earth assured by ransoms paid in the name of Philoctetes, Samson, or Agamemnon."[32] The link to du Fresnois, the core of the first play, is a version of a myth of theater in France as well.

But it is at this juncture that the private myth of Giraudoux joins a remarkable public myth. For the allusions to a combination of extreme Left and Right in the years from 1912 to 1914 in France, snuffed out by the Great War, were extremely resonant in the 1930s. On 16 December 1911, the opening session of the Cercle Proudhon, a fusion of Maurrassian nationalists and Sorelian syndicalists, took place. Their common banner was a violent antidemocratism; their ambitious program, to prepare "the encounter of the two French traditions that were opposed throughout the nineteenth century: nationalism and authentic socialism, not vitiated by democracy, and represented by syndicalism."[33] As one may have surmised from the indications in *Siegfried*, du Fresnois—or Forestier—was a member of the Cercle Proudhon.[34] Now in the 1930s the Cercle was being mythologized by those Frenchmen eager to embrace fascism not as a foreign fascination, but as the renewal of a national tradition.[35] Whence Drieu la Rochelle, quoted at the conclusion of a 1936 article entitled "Fascisme 1913": "it will be seen that several elements of the fascist atmosphere were already united in France toward 1913 before they were elsewhere. There were young men, coming from different social classes, who were animated by the love of heroism and violence and who dreamed of fighting what they called evil on two fronts: capitalism and parliamentary socialism, and reclaiming what was their own from both sides. There were, I believe, at Lyon men who called themselves socialist-royalists or something similar. Already the marriage of nationalism and socialism was projected. Yes, in France, in the vicinity of the Action Française and Péguy, there was the nebula of a kind of fascism."[36] The fundamental link, in Giraudoux's text, between the ascension to power of Zelten and the restoration-resuscitation of Forestier has been observed. It is a relation homologous with that between a certain French solidarity with Hitler and the effort to revive the Cercle Proudhon in the 1930s. Zelten, before abdicating: "They have just caught me in the act of adultery with Germany. Yes, I have slept with her, Siegfried . . ." (p. 59). Robert Brasillach, 19 February 1944: "Frenchmen of any degree of thoughtfulness during these last few years will have more or less slept with Germany, not without strife, and their recollection of it will remain sweet . . ."[37]

Some ten years after *Siegfried*, on the eve of World War II, Giraudoux was to publish the parable of a different Forestier in his tract on urbanism, *Pleins pouvoirs*. For the central chapter in that book, "La France moderne: notre vie," begins with a curious dedicatory fable to a polytechnician and landscape architect named Forestier. The chapter, originally a lecture, is to be a "homage to his memory."[38] Now Forestier's drama was that his passion for creating gardens and delightful public spaces was condemned to be fulfilled throughout the world: "everywhere except in France."[39] His abiding sadness was to see his dreams for Paris reach fruition in Havana, Seville, and Barcelona —for the open space of Paris had been turned over to the pillage of the speculators. The rest of the chapter, in fact, details the losing battle of the defenders of clean air [*l'air libre*] against the moneyed interests [*les entreprises de l'argent*].[40] The chapter, then, has two major series of resonances with the Giraudoux we have already encountered. First, with *Judith*, for the ecological investment in *air libre* serves as the metaphor of Holophernes's resistance to the gods—more specifically to the God of the Jews—insofar as their presence is in a deep sense unhygienic: "It is one of the rare human corners that are truly free. The gods infest our poor universe, Judith. From Greece to the Indies, North to South, there is not a country in which they don't swarm, each with his own vices, his own odors. The atmosphere of the world, for whoever enjoys breathing, is that of a roomful of gods. . . . But there are still a few places forbidden to them . . . recesses of earthly paradise" (p. 277). The association, however, is not only with Holophernes, but with Forestier, in *Siegfried*, as well. For like his homonym, Forestier is a Frenchman condemned to spectacular achievement abroad. Giraudoux's evocation of the depth of the Third Republic's incomprehension of Forestier is worth noting: "This creator, this man overflowing with inventiveness, was called on by our administration, but only to name him the opposite of what he was: a conservationist [*conservateur*, that is: a conservative]."[41] For at about that time, Bernanos, evoking *his* youth in the Cercle Proudhon (the last allegiance of *Siegfried*'s Forestier), resorts to words remarkably parallel to Giraudoux's: "We were not right-wingers [*des gens de droite*]. The circle for social studies we had founded bore the name Cercle Proudhon, flaunted that scandalous affiliation . . ."[42] Neither "right-wing" nor "conservative," Forestier 1939, like Bernanos—or Forestier 1913 —evinces a radicalism in his anticapitalism that is as well the mark of Giraudoux's text.

The chapter ends with reference to Paris "manipulated by that elusive and irresponsible oligarchy which dominates our urbanism as it does our demography . . ."[43] In urbanism as in demography, there is a common enemy. It is, in fact, on matters demographic, the subject of the book's previous chapter, "La France peuplée," that *Pleins pouvoirs* sounds its most radical note. It is there that, in terms of *Siegfried*, we revert from Forestier to Zelten. For the "sole" French problem, we are told, is the problem of race.[44] On the one hand, there is a declining birthrate ("the slow plague"); but on the other, a refusal to control the immigration of racial undesirables, principally the Jews.[45] "Our land has become a land invaded. The invasion is conducted in exactly the same manner as in the Roman Empire, not by armies, but by a continuous infiltration of Barbarians."[46] The publication of such sentences gives some indication of the severe dilemma Giraudoux, in the best of cases, would be faced with the following year when France was invaded *by* the would-be heirs of the Roman Empire. In fact, though, Giraudoux's position in the chapter is consistent with that of the literary works we have examined thus far. Here, then, is a representative passage on the Jews from *Pleins pouvoirs*:

There have entered into our land, through an infiltration whose secret I have
in vain attempted to discover, about one hundred thousand Ashkenasis,
escaped from the ghettos of Poland or Rumania, whose spiritual discipline
—but not whose particularism—they reject. Trained as they have been for
centuries to work in the worst conditions, they eliminate our compatriots
—while destroying their professional customs and traditions—from all the
crafts of artisanry: clothing, footwear, furs, leather, and, piled up by tens
in single rooms, escape every investigation relating to the census, taxes,
and labor. All these emigrants, accustomed to living in the margins of the
State and to avoiding its laws, accustomed to dodging all the burdens of
tyranny, have no difficulty in eluding those of freedom; they bring wherever
they pass a sense of imprecision, secrecy, misappropriation, corruption,
and are constant threats to the spirit of exactitude, good faith and perfection
that was characteristic of French artisanry. A horde which manages to be
deprived of all its national rights and to defy every expulsion and whose
precarious and abnormal physical constitution sends it, by the thousands,
into our hospitals, that it encumbers.[47]

Thus is the Frenchman crowded—or swindled—out of his own garden.
For the Frenchman is Edenic: "his rule of life . . . rather resembles
that which must have guided the first humans created, if their garden
and dress were such as they have been depicted: a kind of refinement
of tone."[48] One possible recourse might well be, then, that other deni-
zen of Eden, with his mixture of candor and genocide, Holophernes:
"a man at last of this world. The first, if you like . . . the friend of
gardens in bloom . . ." (p. 278). Giraudoux concludes: "only a Ministry of Race holds the key to the well-being of France." Whereupon a
salute to the contemporary statesman best attuned to the truth of his
chapter: "We are fully in agreement with Hitler in proclaiming that a
politics attains its superior form only if it is racial . . ."[49]

It is perhaps one measure of the desperation of the French situation
in 1939, as perceived by Giraudoux, that the framing conceit of the
chapter "Nos Travaux" is a letter from a madman, proposing public
works—including a series of "rainbow monuments"—each marked
by a measure of insanity. The letter allows the author to pay tribute
to the frenetic public achievements of France's totalitarian neighbors,
and to affirm that a valid moral and/or material public works project
is, essentially, imbued with a touch of delirium. For only a measure
of madness will propel a nation into a future of monumental achievement. It is that suggestion which allows us to suspend at this juncture
this first set of prolegomena—we shall present others—to a reading of

La Folle de Chaillot. A final reference to *Siegfried*, or to a scene de-
leted from it, will allow us to anticipate the impetus of that reading.
Tourism, we are told in *Pleins pouvoirs*, is an exemplary *grand travail*,
and the preeminent tourist of France is the Frenchman. Now there is
a curious interlude of farce involving the art of French tourism in the
abandoned initial version of the final act of *Siegfried*. To ease Forestier's return to France, an extravagant old Frenchwoman is commissioned to summon all the French residents of Munich to the hero's
side: "It's a matter of surrounding someone, it seems, with a nice little
French atmosphere [*une bonne petite atmosphère française*]."[50] With
her crew of zanies—in this case mostly *porcelainiers*—she will make
her final appearance in Giraudoux as the Madwoman of Chaillot. Her
project this time is thwarted by the assassination of Siegfried. But it
will be perceived that the liberating touch of madness that was to take
France—through its *grands travaux*—into the 1940s (*Pleins pouvoirs*)
was already at work, in the service of Zelten's (failed) revolution, attempting to restore Forestier to his origins in the protofascist formation of 1913. Indeed the future effort might even redeem the failure
of the first. Such indeed will be the achievement of *Siegfried's vieille
dame*, reemergent as *La Folle*.

II

The common attribution to Giraudoux of two Biblical (or "Hebraic")
plays, *Judith* (1931) and *Sodome et Gomorrhe* (1943), constitutes a
curious oversight of his one-act modern-dress *Cantique des cantiques*,
first performed in 1938. True, *Song of Songs* is something of an anom-
aly in the Scriptures itself. But it is precisely that anomalous quality
which rendered it a perfect subject for Giraudoux. Consider, first, that
it is a splash of barely manageable eroticism disfiguring the Sacred
Text. Herein lay its profound affinity with *Judith*. That eroticism,
moreover, is marked by a fundamental split. For the exegetes have
long hesitated between two interpretations of what is essentially a sequence of love poems. Are there *two* characters—Solomon and his
Shulamite bride—indulging in expressions of mutual love? Or are
there *three*: an enamored Solomon, the Shulamite maiden, and her
shepherd lover, for whom she rejects the king?[51] At the core of the
text, then, is the kind of surprising duplication of the couple that
Mauron, as we saw, discovered as the node of the general economy

of Giraudoux's theater: e.g., Electre-Oreste/Clytemnestre-Egisthe, but Forestier-Geneviève/Siegfried-Eva as well. Ultimately, the interpretation of the Biblical text consists in the attribution of dramatic roles to sections of a protracted poetic cycle. It is a task not without parallels to the abstraction of Giraudoux's first play, *Siegfried*, from what is in many ways a long prose poem on Germany, *Siegfried et le Limousin*. A final factor that must have recommended the text to Giraudoux's sympathies is the tradition of allegorical interpretation whereby first the Jews (in the Targum), then the Christians (Origen) were to resacralize its erotic contents. For the subject of those allegories—the history of Israel, or Christ in the Church—is a version of the *choix-des-élues* motif which we have already seen in *Judith* and which would eventually give its title to his novel of 1939.

Giraudoux's play takes place on the terrace of a luxurious café. A "President" awaits his mistress, Florence, for a rendez-vous only to be greeted by a fatuous young man, Jérôme, who announces that as Florence's *fiancé*, he is delighted to meet the gentleman whom she admires more than any other. The bulk of the play consists of the final meeting between the President and Florence, during which, she—the Shulamite—details to her Solomon the mediocrity and inferiority of the "shepherd" lover for whom she will nevertheless leave him. "For such is love, no? It's only that, but that *is* indeed what it is. As for him, I don't love him. That's evident. But it is love . . . ." (p. 227)[52] The President, a man of consummate urbanity, agrees. Florence leaves with Jérôme.

Now the most intense section of the play concerns Florence's return to the President of jewels he had given her. For in the course of their return, the President manages to bestow them upon her once again. He reoffers them to her less as testimony to his affection than as some final relation—be it metaphorical—to the indifference she is about to abandon as she is swallowed up by what even she perceives as the pervasive mediocrity of her love. The stones, she is told, are poor pretexts for any indulgence of sentiment. "They are your shares of indifference . . . your impassive parts. You don't have too many. Don't let them escape. . . . Take this clasp. It's a diamond. It is impassiveness itself " (p. 234). These pockets of indifference that stud her skin, tokens of a curious intersubjectivity—or exchange—without sentiment, are eventually accepted, not only as protection against Jérôme's fatuousness, but as withering evidence of the President's cruelty as well: "You

insist on proving to yourself that I'm a coward, on proving it to me.
. . . Very well. I accept them" (p. 237). As the jewels, returned, re-
accepted, refract the ultimate intensities of the text, they function
almost as a rudimentary figure of the unconscious, Giraudoux's own
effort to organize his text around a mobile battery of irreducible elements, fundamentally resistant to psychological analysis.

It is for this reason that I would attach special importance to the
fact that the episode of the return of the jewels in 1938 is, in fact, the
return of a sequence from Giraudoux's novel of 1927, *Eglantine*. Eglantine is a passive young beauty, a figure of Fate, who in the center of
the novel has a protracted—and disinterested—romance with a like-
able but physically repulsive Jewish banker named Moïse. He is a reg-
ular—and grotesque—*habitué* of a society swimming club, we have already learned from Giraudoux's previous novel *Bella*, and is regularly
rescued, midst affectionate jeering, from the pool. *Moïse sauvé des
eaux*: his Moses is ultimately as ironically conceived as Forestier's
Siegfried. Now Moïse's delight in bestowing jewels on his beloved is
identical to the President's in *Cantique des cantiques*. Moïse, after his
first gift of a ring, "saw the slight bump beneath the chamois, and
watched, with emotion, Eglantine disappear, almost pregnant by him,
pregnant with a pearl."[53] Similarly, the President recalls: "With a
heavy heart I watched you disappear, almost pregnant by me, pregnant
with a pearl" (p. 235). The parallel even includes an abbreviated version of the failed return of the jewels to the President: "All the jewels
gradually returned to her person, in a perfect arrangement . . ."[54] The
President, then, is at some level the banker Moïse of the 1927 novel.
But Moïse's identity is entirely a function of his difference from another character in *Eglantine*, Fontranges. For Fontranges, the aged
and slightly hapless aristocrat, is the person for whom Eglantine leaves
Moïse, the counterpart of Jérôme in the later work. The opposition,
crudely, is between "the last of the Crusaders" and "the millionaire."[55]
Whereas Moïse bedecks Eglantine with jewels, Fontranges, on a crucial
occasion, bestows on her a transfusion of his blood.[56] Nowhere, however, is the difference between the two—ultimately between Occident
and Orient—more elaborately present than in Giraudoux's evocation
of the circumstance that convinces the heroine to abandon Moïse for
Fontranges. One day she sees Fontranges toss a salad, and realizes all
that distinguishes him from her other suitor. The ease with which Fontranges performs reminds her of her embarrassment at Moïse's pathetic

extortion of flattery from his guests whenever he acquits himself of that task: "She swallowed her salad regretfully, as though it were the dish of another race, suddenly felt herself carnivorous, and averted her eyes from those of Moïse . . ."[57] Even the god/man opposition, the stuff of Giraudoux's tragedies, is fed into the evocation of Fontranges's *saladier*: the preparation, we read, "was in no manner religious: the oil, which was walnut, was not poured from Richelieu's cruet, but from a common dispenser."[58] In brief, it is enough for Eglantine to witness Fontranges in his garden of lettuce for her to feel herself the "slave of a pasha."[59] Whereupon she breaks her chains, abandons Moïse.

Now the novel ends with the agonizing description of Eglantine and Fontranges in bed on the crucial occasion of her realization that he has no erotic interest in her: "He who honored unformulated pledges, fulfilled unmade wishes, respected inexistent spouses, for whom there had assembled, around this girl, unbound, who offered herself, every invisible and insurmountable obstacle—he wanted nothing of her, rejected her."[60] The novel ends with her staring at him sleeping with something of the attitude of Psyche, we are told, something of the violence of Judith, we suspect.

The Jew, then, has been discomfited only for his conqueror to be vanquished by his own sexual insufficiency. Blood has defeated Money only to falter in the face of Sex.[61] Now in the structure of the novel, Fontranges's impotence is superimposable on Jérôme's fatuousness. The aristocrat and the worker, in fact, have much in common. Of Jérôme, Florence observes that he has no imagination. Of the aged Fontranges, we read in *Bella*: "it was the first metaphor to have ever traversed the brow of Fontranges."[62] Jérôme is said to have his future in mechanics or electricity, but his shallowness has some of the quasi-Heideggerian simplicity of the distracted provincial nobleman: "In life, what does he do? . . . Nothing. He is there [*il est là*]: that's his trade. . . . He endlessly studies the weather [*le temps*], meticulously. . . ." (p. 224). The superimposition of worker (Jérôme) and aristocrat (Fontranges), opposed to the Jew-politician (Moïse, the President), was in fact the Sorelian fantasy that fueled (Forestier's) Cercle Proudhon. The specificity of Giraudoux's version would seem to lie in the apparent irrelevance even of its victory. There is an (admittedly endearing) thinness to Jérôme and Fontranges, whose most painful manifestation is impotence. Their every triumph—in Hector's terms, in *La Guerre de Troie*—seems part of a more fundamental defeat. In the face of which, desperate measures might be needed. Again we have followed the intricacies of Giraudoux's text to the point where they open on to *La Folle de Chaillot*. That play begins on a café terrace. Seated is a character called "Le Président." It is virtually the opening of *Cantique des cantiques*. One further set of prolegomena, and we will be prepared to engage *La Folle* itself.

III

Sodome et Gomorrhe, Giraudoux's final Biblical play, first performed during the Occupation in 1943, knew a considerable success, and was in fact playing on the day of the author's death, 31 January 1944. With its prologue about "the end of the world," the death of empires, the play has been interpreted—vaguely—as an expression of the pessimism marking the author in his final years. Giraudoux's drama, moreover, which deals with the bitter dissolution of the—or a—last couple, has been interpreted biographically as testimony of the desperation of the Giraudoux *ménage*. It is precisely this apparently psychological question of the couple, however, that will allow us to envision an articulation of Giraudoux's text—by way of "literary history"—with broader questions normally consigned to history "proper." The play, then, deals with the breakup not simply of the last couple, but of the ideal couple, Jean and Lia, versions of Giraudoux's Edenic—or first—pair. It seems organized fundamentally around the enigma that Lia voices in act 2: "The secret of this defect. The vice of the couple God wanted and made the most loving, loyal, and healthy. He is like us. He doesn't understand. Why that crevice suddenly fissured our happiness. Why I quarrel with the only man I agree with, hate the only man I love, flee the only one for whom I feel no aversion" (p. 61).[63] She asks Jean whether he understands, and he responds in kind. Their fated separation is in spite of her, in spite of him. It is precisely this situation that suggests to Mauron that Giraudoux, no doubt, had Racine's *Bérénice*—"a purely psychological tragedy," with minimal plot—in mind when writing his play.[64] "*Invitus invitam*," as Racine was to quote Suetonius at the beginning of his preface. That suggestion of Giraudoux writing a *Bérénice* 1943—in the wake, moreover, of Brasillach's *Bérénice* of 1940, *La Reine de Césarée*—should give us pause.[65] For Racine's subject is the agonizing decision of Emperor Titus, conqueror of Judea, to exile his Jewish love, Bérénice, because she is Jewish, in spite of his wishes, in spite of hers, out of a presumed sense of allegiance to the duties of Empire newly incumbent upon him. Imagine, then, Giraudoux reading Racine in occupied Paris or in his country home at Cusset, just outside Vichy . . .

Titus appears initially to Bérénice as a would-be conqueror of the Jews, Holophernes *redivivus*: "Il parut devant vous dans tout l'éclat d'un homme / Qui porte entre ses mains la vengeance de Rome. / La Judée en pâlit . . ."[66] The backdrop of the play must have seemed particularly uncanny in 1943. Bérénice: "Ces flambeaux, ce bûcher, cette nuit enflammée / Ces aigles, ces faisceaux, ce peuple, cette armée"[67] Midst the iconography resurgent in fascism comes the racial imperative. Paulin: "Rome, par une loi qui ne se peut changer, / N'admet avec son sang aucun sang étranger."[68] The expulsion-deportation of the Jewess is, in fact, the popular mandate, claims Bérénice, of "un peuple injurieux / Qui fait de mon malheur retentir tous ces lieux. / Ne l'entendez-vous pas, cette cruelle joie, / Tandis que dans les pleurs, moi seule, je me noie? / Quel crime, quelle offense a pu les animer?"[69] Deportation, she realizes at the brink of desperation, is tantamount to death: "Titus m'aime. Titus ne veut point que je meure."[70] Our quotations, admittedly selective, already allow us to affirm that it was impossible for Giraudoux to read—and rewrite—*Bérénice* in the early 1940s without perceiving its relation to the drama of French Jewry at the time. Vichy published its first "statut des Juifs" in October 1940. The last convoy left Drancy for Auschwitz in July 1944. In between, 76,000 Jews were deported to the East with the consent of the French government.[71] It would appear, then, that through Bérénice we are again engaging the motif of Aryan and Jew in Giraudoux.

We turn now to Titus, or rather to the embarrassment he has traditionally constituted throughout the history of the play's interpretation. For all his protestations, audiences have been hard put to believe in Titus's love. Thus already Bussy Rabutin in a letter to Madame Bossuet: "It appears to me that Titus does not love her as much as he claims, since he makes no effort on her behalf with the Senate and Roman populace . . ." And later Rousseau: "Titus can remain Roman if he likes, he is alone in his decision; the entire audience has married Bérénice . . ."[72] The suspicion of hypocrisy, then, weighs heavily on his character, as though he were faking a sacrifice while pursuing a project secretly his own. Mauron, describing Bérénice as "truly unhappy" and Titus as "falsely Cornelian," captures this nicely.[73]

At this juncture, however, with the question of Titus's autonomy and/or hypocrisy in his new relation to the Empire and his deportation of the Jewess, we appear to be engaging an allegory of contemporary historical research. For the upshot of M. Marrus and R. Paxton's important book on Vichy and the Jews is that contrary to received opinion, on the question of Jewish policy, Vichy was not the slave of the German Reich, but the enthusiastic architect of its own autonomous anti-Semitism, replete with an elaborate bureaucracy.[74] Maurice Druon in February 1977 evoked "that unfortunate period in which the laws of the Occupant were accepted, *hélàs*, by a captive State."[75] It is the *hélàs* of Racine's Titus. Against which, we would set Mauron's reading of Titus, or Paxton's conclusion on Vichy: "the new political personnel promulgated an anti-Semitism *in rivalry and competition with* German anti-Semitism. The publication of the first 'Statut des Juifs' was a French initiative."[76] To be interpreting—or rewriting—*Bérénice* in 1943 was to anticipate and encounter the structure of Paxton and Marrus's conclusions in 1981.

Mauron on Titus: "The almost unanimous impression was that he was lacking in ardor, perhaps in masculinity."[77] Let that evocation of flagging virility serve as a transition to *Sodome et Gomorrhe*. For Giraudoux's reading of Racine is essentially Mauron's. If the woman here (Lia) chooses to break with the man (Jean), it is because she is all too aware of the shallowness—or hypocrisy—of his commitment. Lia: "Jean has a flying carpet. When, in earlier years, there arose between us too great a love, then too great an indifference, Jean climbed on his carpet and took off. He still flies it in his hatred . . ." (p. 21). Such is, in fact, the "generous scorn" [*dépit*] that will characterize the abandoned Bérénice's desire to leave Rome on her own schedule at the end of Racine's play (1265). Giraudoux's Lia in some ways begins where Bérénice leaves off. Jean, like Titus, is revealed to be essentially a *poseur*. Thus Lia: "How barren and commonplace man is in the face of duty. . . . Your woman comes to you, begging, flayed, adulterous, and that's all you tell her, all you ask of her: to pose with you for the portrait that will show future generations Jean and Lia receiving death . . ." (p. 72). The drama of the couple evoked in *Sodome et Gomorrhe* is essentially that discussed by Mauron in his chapter on *Bérénice*.[78] Despite appearances, the male seems always already in flight from his partner.

If *Sodome et Gomorrhe* may be read as a rewriting of *Bérénice*, it is simultaneously a recasting of Giraudoux's first Biblical drama, *Judith*. That play had Judith moving through a series of stages she was hard put to reach and overcome. First, the discovery of the lack of substance of her *fiancé*, Jean; then, her idyllic night culminating in the murder of Holophernes; and finally, her subjugation by the Angel (in the form of a guard) who inflicts God's truth on her. Lia appears to rush desperately through those stages, meeting little resistance at each. She too abandons a Jean but has already chosen the Angel before she even begins her flirtation with Jacques. Jacques, in the position of Holophernes, actually resembles the hapless Jérôme of *Cantique des cantiques*. Thus Lia: "Oh Angel, if you really think I don't foresee what my life with Jacques will be . . ." (p. 43). By the end of act 1 the Angel, who had conquered Judith in act 3 of *her* play, has been propositioned by Lia, and the rest of the play simply allows the audience to catch up with Lia and the position she had arrived at almost from the outset.

In terms of *Littérature*, we encounter, then, between *Sodome* and *Judith* the relation of repetition-*déchaînement* posited between Laclos and Racine. The positions of *Judith*'s structure are present, but unable to retain any identity in the face of Lia's frenzy. She follows "a streak of combustion," a "straight line" that burns through the structure, issuing in a collapse simultaneous with the collapse of France (p. 62). The Angel, who resists Lia's embrace, qualifies her situation as a kind of generalized renunciation of everything—trees, meadows, beasts at play—given man to distract him from his soliloquy and his sin, to impede an undue communion with self. His diatribe concludes: "Your occupation is yourself" [*Ton occupation, c'est toi-même*] (p. 40). We would perhaps do well to think less in terms of narcissism here than of the—related—concept of the death instinct, unbinding structures, obstacles, and difference itself in its rush back to homogeneity.[79] For Freud, masochism was primary in that "instinct." For Giraudoux's Lia, it is ultimate. What she asks of the Angel is "the supreme pleasure of not having any," the pleasure of pleasure's absence—or masochism (p. 44).

"Ton occupation, c'est toi-même," says the Angel in the passage just quoted. May we not intuit some resonance with the Occupation of France, the preponderant historical reality during the writing of the play? Consider that *Judith* is a drama of Judaization. The Jews snatch the encounter of Judith with the Aryan back into their theology. If

Sodome offers in Lia a repetition and exacerbation of Judith's progress, at some level it constitutes an even more frenetically pursued Judaization. We have already seen Giraudoux, in *Pleins pouvoirs*, just prior to the German invasion, talk about an "invasion" by the Jews. Drieu la Rochelle, in the *N.R.F.* of August 1941, sounds a similar note: "Four million foreigners in France, a million of them Jews, gave me long before you [Germans] a sense of the horrors of occupation."[80] And what if the term "occupation," at the beginning of this paragraph, addressed to Lia (behind whom, Bérénice) were used in Drieu's sense? The impotence of Fontranges in *Eglantine*, the shallowness of Jérôme in *Cantique*, are indications of the abject weakness of the anti-Jew in France. The "end of the world" mentioned in the prologue is generally taken to allude to the fall of France. By the end of the play, however, Abraham and Sarah may be seen rushing "through the debris" [*entre les décombres*] to safety (p. 76). *Les Décombres* was, of course, the title of Rebatet's anti-Semitic bestseller about the collapse of the Third Republic. The end of the "French world" is thus imagined as a beginning of the Jewish one. In the face of which, even the panicky deportations of Titus, Jean's prototype, may prove paltry. A more radical solution is called for, and its substance is the implict matter of *La Folle de Chaillot*.

IV

Louis Jouvet, in his comments on the initial performance of *La Folle de Chaillot*, was careful to insist that the text of the posthumous play had been rewritten and corrected several times over by the author.[81] This was, no doubt, to counter the general suspicion that Giraudoux had not completed his text. To all appearances, the suspicion had some basis. For the typical schema of the Giraudoux play lay in exploiting that level of latency in a received myth or truth at which its relations—of power—had not yet been reversed and consolidated into the form in which myth or truth has become familiar to us. Judith was imagined as stripped of all sense of her Judaism, the Trojan War as not—necessarily—taking place. Indeed *Sodome et Gomorrhe*'s subject might well be summarized as *La-fin-du-monde-n'aura-pas-lieu*. The author's ethical and aesthetic visions coincide in elaborating that level of imaginative freedom prior to the fatal reversal operated by the myth. His rhetoric is ultimately one of chiasmus. Of this scheme, little

had apparently survived in *La Folle*. Whence the suspicion of incompletion.

What follows will be a reading of Giraudoux's play based on the implications of the prolegomena presented above, and arriving at a *virtual
construct* of the play wholly in accord with the chiasmic scheme just
described. As if the motif of "prospection" in the play were an invitation to excavate a different text which Giraudoux's fantasy of 1943
silently reverses.

La Folle opens on the sidewalk of the café Francis in the Place de
l'Alma. A President hosts a meeting with a Baron (then a Broker
[*Coulissier*], and a Prospector), whose aim is the formation of a business combine for the exploitation of oil deposits beneath Paris. The
Prospector has blackmailed a young man [*jeune garçon*], Pierre, to
blow up the house of a refractory engineer. He attempts suicide instead and ultimately falls into the hands of the enemies of the syndi-
cate, the crew of neighborhood zanies forever interrupting the combine's operations. He becomes one of them. The countersyndicate is
led by an imposing and extravagant old woman, La Folle de Chaillot.
Her most eloquent associate in the plan they together hatch is the
Ragpicker [*Chiffonnier*]. That plan consists in luring the would-be
speculators to a sewer from which there is no return on the pretext
that it contains an oil deposit worthy of their inspection. The second
act consists largely of the preparation and execution of the Madwoman's plan: the mass extermination of the speculators. At play's end,
the Madwoman has saved Paris, and Pierre has discovered love with
the local dishwasher, Irma.

We shall first recall the principal links with the works examined
thus far:

1. The motif of the anticapitalist revolution—imbued with local
tradition and short on rationality—we first encountered in Zelten, in
the novelistic prototext of *Siegfried*. In the first version of the play, his
plans were solidary with those of the old Frenchwoman commissioned
to surround Forestier with all the prototypically French residents of
Munich, in preparation for his return to his French origins. *La Folle*—
as Mauron, following other indexes, speculated—brings off Zelten's
aborted *coup*.

2. From the Forestier of *Siegfried*, we moved to his homonym in
Pleins pouvoirs. The urban ills described in the earlier tract are essentially those against which the posthumous play militates: a *mafia* of

"pimps" exploiting everything in sight. A touch of delirium was said to lie at the core of the *grands travaux* that might ease the blight. Suffice it to say that in act 2 Aurélie, the Madwoman, is accorded "pleins pouvoirs" to resolve matters (p. 164).[82]

3. *La Folle de Chaillot*, like *Cantique des cantiques*, begins with "the President" awaiting an assignation on the terrace of a café. "The President," then, is at some level the same in the two plays. *Cantique des cantiques* appeared originally in a double bill with *Tricolore*, by Giraudoux's friend Pierre Lestringuez. That play, quoted by some as a "source" for *La Folle*, is centered on a minor heroine of the French Revolution, Théroigne de Méricourt, "the Amazon of Liberty."[83] Hence the links between *La Folle* and *Cantique* are substantial. We have traced the President of *Cantique*, however, to the quintessentially Jewish banker, Moïse, the Orient incarnate. This clinches a hypothesis already sustained by the previous links: the group whose extermination the play celebrates in 1943 is the Jews.

The principal contribution that *Sodome et Gomorrhe* affords at this juncture is the reminder of the relevance of Racine to the problematic of Aryan and Jew in Giraudoux. Deportation, glimpsed through the intertext of *Bérénice*, is a transitional stage to liquidation. Racine and his repetition, in fact, had been at the heart of the literary tradition that *was* the history Giraudoux, in 1941, would bring to succor his compatriots in their hour of distress. The return of Racine in *Littérature*, moreover, entailed a secret act of revenge. Of the two protagonists of *Les Liaisons dangéreuses*, we read: "a greater poet would have intimated to us whom they were avenging; Laclos may not have "known" (p. 65). Giraudoux's own answer, the conclusion of his essay, is the list of Racinian heroines, beginning with Andromaque, quoted in our reading of *Judith*. He stops short of Racine's final heroine, qualified in the "Racine" essay as Andromaque "in gray hair" and "the old lady" [*la vieillarde*] (p. 45). And yet it is Athalie, we shall see, whose fate is reversed in *La Folle de Chaillot*.

Athalie pits the Jewish potentate, Joad, against the horrendous "vieillarde," Athalie. She is criminal queen of Judea, worshiper of Baal, and on the verge of consolidating her shaky right to the throne by massacring the Jews. Whence the almost Jonestown-like air of hysteria that gives the play its predominant note. Act 3, scene 7, for instance, ends with a choral mobilization of the Jews preparing for martyrdom:

> Hélas! si pour venger l'opprobre d'Israël,
> Nos mains ne peuvent pas, comme autrefois Jahel,
> Des ennemis de Dieu percer la tête impie,
> Nous lui pouvons du moins immoler notre vie.[84]

In fact, however, it is Joad and the God of Israel who will triumph in the end. For the play, it has been observed, is constructed like an elaborate trap into which the evil heroine is drawn.[85] At play's end, she is lured into the temple by a false promise of treasure, and succumbs to the Levites organized by Joad around young Joas-Eliacin, revealed to be a member of the royal line saved from Athalie's earlier violence. Athalie has fallen into the trap; the Jews emerge victorious. She is murdered in the wings.

Now the psychological richness of the play lies in Athalie's ambivalent attraction toward the young Joas. She has learned in her celebrated dream that a young boy will kill her, and she subsequently recognizes him in the Temple. Nevertheless, she remains secretly and intensely attracted to him. It is ultimately her kindness to him that will seal her death. The aged *délirante* and her prepubescent boy (in fact, her grandson)—such is the final figure assumed by the couple of Phèdre and Hippolyte.

A final chapter of importance in the play is Mathan, the villain [*traître*]. He has deserted the Hebrews and followed the path of power to Athalie, whose counselor in genocide he has become.

> Moi seul, donnant l'exemple aux timides Hébreux,
> Déserteur de leur loi, j'approuvai l'entreprise,
> Et par là de Baal méritai la prêtrise . . .[86]

His is the psychology of Collaboration.

Return to *La Folle* with *Athalie*. In each case we find the Jews threatened by a deeply disturbed woman—unsuccessfully in Racine, successfully in Giraudoux. Athalie's first appearance is evoked by Joad's son:

> Dans un parvis, aux hommes réservé,
> Cette femme superbe entre, le front levé
> Et se préparait même à passer les limites
> De l'enceinte sacrée . . .
>
> . . .
>
> Mon Père . . . Ah! quel courroux animait ses regards!
>
> . . .

> "Reine, sors, a-t-il dit, de ce lieu redoutable . . ."
> La reine alors, sur lui jetant un oeil farouche,
> Pour blasphémer sans doute ouvrait déjà la bouche . . .[87]

Whereupon she sees Eliacin, is reduced to stunned silence, and leaves. And now Aurélie, arriving at the café: "The Madwoman of Chaillot appears. *En grande dame*" (p. 102). Her extravagant dress is described; she engages in a brief exchange with Irma. Whereupon: "She reflects, takes a step forward, stops in front of the President's table." The President reacts with Joad's sense of outrage: "Waiter, get this woman out of here!" [*faites circuler cette femme*]. He is rebuffed, told she is *chez elle*. Her final gesture before leaving the stage consists of deliberately emptying the President's glass on his trousers.

The principal psychological tension in Racine's plot concerns Athalie's relations with the diminutive Eliacin, the future of the royal line. She first sees him in her dream:

> . . . lorsque, revenant de mon trouble funeste
> J'admirais sa douceur, son air noble et modeste,
> J'ai senti tout à coup un homicide acier
> Que le traître en mon sein a plongé tout entier.[88]

She next sees him in the Temple, is struck by his grace:

> Quel prodige nouveau me trouble et m'embarrasse?
> La douceur de sa voix, son enfance, sa grâce,
> Font insensiblement à mon inimitié
> Succéder . . . Je serais sensible à la pitié?[89]

She invites the orphan to her palace, is rebuffed, becomes desperate:

> Je veux vous faire part de toutes mes richesses
> . . .
> Je prétends vous traiter comme mon propre fils.[90]

Compare now the Madwoman's relation to Pierre, the somewhat inane and degenerate figure of a Giralducian hero. Like Eliacin-Joas, he is given two names—La Folle: "Call him Fabrice. It's noon. At noon, all men are called Fabrice" (p. 113). Aurélie intuits falsely the act of violence that drove Pierre to suicide: "I realize why you threw yourself into the river, Fabrice. . . . Because the Prospector asked you . . . to kill me" (p. 115). This divination betrays the anecdote of the play, but reproduces the configuration of Athalie's dream. The filial relation is evoked by Irma, one of Aurélie's confederates: "And if it were her son that she just found . . ." (p. 120). Finally, the Madwoman's relation to Pierre is marked by a curious erotic displacement. If she refuses to release him, it is because forty years earlier she allowed her beloved Adolphe Bertaut to abandon her. Whence her madness . . . To all these pleas, Pierre responds as did Joas: "Let me go [*lâchez-moi*], Madame!"—until he is won over by the values of her band (p. 119). In brief, the source of Athalie's downfall—an enigmatic sympathy for the boy and would-be son she has dreamed as her killer—accrues to the benefit of Aurélie, once she has won him away from the Jews. It is ultimately *she* who will bestow on him that latter-day version of a scepter—Irma, a pert French bride.

Mathan, we have seen, is the Collaborator, the deserter of the Hebrews who has become the most hawkish advocate of their extermination. Consider him in relation to the Ragpicker, the important role first played by Jouvet. For in act 2, a mock trial is held in Aurélie's kangaroo court, in which the Ragpicker chooses to defend the rich by speaking as one of them: "I'm the ideal rich man. I'm not particularly proud of it, but that's how it is" (p. 158). Now by dint of Giraudoux's virtuosity, the Ragpicker's impersonation of a millionaire soon gets out of hand, and he begins a rather brutal seduction of Irma, the woman whose coupling with Pierre Aurélie's entire plot—as well as Giraudoux's play—is intended to ensure. The hint of treasonous collaboration in this case does not work—successfully—with the Jew's enemies, as in Racine, but only partially, unsuccessfully, and with the Jews (i.e., the capitalists). On the other hand, consider the Ragpicker's discourse in act 1 in light of the category of collaboration: "It's an invasion, Countess. In the old days, when you traveled about Paris, the people you met were like yourself, they were yourself. . . . But one day, ten years ago already, in the street, something turned my stomach. Among the passers-by, I saw a man who had nothing in common with the usual crowd: thickset, potbellied, the right eye brazen, the left eye anxious, a different race. He walked with plenty of room, but in a curious way, threatening, uneasy, as though he had killed one of my *habitués* in order to take his place. He *had* killed him. He was the first one. The invasion was beginning" (p. 124). The reader recognizes a motif we encountered in *Pleins pouvoirs*. The Ragpicker, then, is something of a spokesman for Giraudoux in the play. But consider, in that case, that in 1943, with Paris occupied, invaded by the Nazis, Giraudoux was lamenting the invasion of Paris by an alien race of speculators . . . From a consideration of Mathan's psychology of collaboration, we thus move to the Ragpicker's inspired variations on a theme by Hitler. It is one of the most winning roles in the play.

Need we continue the reverse parallel? Joas trembles at the thought of a "holocaust"; Joséphine, Aurélie's confederate, sketches a death camp: "You gather all your enemies in the same place, and you kill them" (p. 152). Even as the *décor* of *Athalie* evolves into a gigantic trap for the heroine, *La Folle*'s final act centers on the planning of a fatal lure for the capitalists. Thus Joad:

> . . . dès que cette reine, ivre d'un fol orgueil,
> De la porte du temple aura passé le seuil,
> Qu'elle ne pourra plus retourner en arrière.[91]

And the sewer tender, explaining his trick sewer to Aurélie: "the steps are so made that you can descend them easily, but you can't climb back up . . ." (p. 135). The bait in each case is to be treasure: King David's gold to lure Athalie, imaginary oil to lure the capitalists.

As Racine's play ends, Athalie is slaughtered, Eliacin-Joas recognized as king, and the future of the Jews secured. As Giraudoux's reaches its conclusion, the (Jew-)capitalists—the President, Moïse, and Company—are exterminated, and Pierre, at Aurélie's urging, forms a (French) couple with Irma: "Embrace each other! Quickly . . . or it will be too late" (p. 179). For the would-be champion of a Ministry of Race, there could be no more crucially political bit of advice than that counsel. The security of France lay in the balance.[92]

V

The Jews: rejected (*Cantique* with *Eglantine*); deported (*Sodome* with *Bérénice*); exterminated (*La Folle* with *Athalie*). Such is the cortege of texts—in 1938, 1943, 1944—with which Giraudoux would defend and illustrate the jeopardized essence of "French literature." The program implicit in the plays—ultimately Holophernes's—grows increasingly grisly, increasingly precise as it secretly celebrates France's role in Europe's inferno. The path into history, it may be noted, is inseparable from the intertextuality of literary history: the more contemporary it becomes, the more it engages the detail of Racine's text. Until, in *La Folle*—*vieillarde* for *vieillarde*—the program invades the very core of Giraudoux's play. In relation to which, the minor gestures

in the direction of collaboration (a manifesto, rejected by Pétain, for
"Une Dictaure de l'urbanisme") or resistance (the sarcasms of *Sans
pouvoirs*) pale into insignificance.[93] Giraudoux's "history" was indeed
"literary," but in a sense of both terms that critical thought has yet to
elaborate. "A literary consciousness singularly unrelated to the anxi-
eties, deliria, and projects of annihilation of the modern age."[94] Thus
Blanchot on Giraudoux's rhetoric in what must appear, in light of our
reading, as a critical exemplum of the psychical defense of denial.
Sartre, at about the time Giraudoux began thinking of *La Folle*, wrote
of a totally metaphysical "schizophrenia" as the aesthetic style of the
author's vision, only to conclude: "M. Giraudoux's profundity is real,
but it is valid for his world, not ours."[95] And if Giraudoux's insanity
were Europe's own? If the cortege of rejection, deportation, and extermination—Giraudoux's practical celebration of the "mission" of
Littérature—were to culminate in 1945 *as* the "liberation" of the Parisian theater? Such is the horizon opened up by a consideration of the
postwar legacy of France's most polished ideologue of its literature;
such the burden that performance of his most popular play entails.

IV.

"JEWISH LITERATURE"
AND THE ART OF ANDRÉ GIDE

The several pages that Gide, in 1938, devoted to Céline's *Bagatelles pour un massacre* are generally regarded as a regrettable, though understandable, error.[1] At a time when the Left was breaking with the much admired author of *Voyage au bout de la nuit*, when Léon Daudet, in a grandiose page, was saluting a monumental advance in France's great prose tradition—Toussenel, Drumont—of Jew-hating, Gide elegently opined that both sides had committed a category error.[2] *Bagatelles* was not so much an anti-Semitic volume as a parody of anti-Semitism: Céline "is doing his best not to be taken seriously."[3] The critics' error, that is, was aesthetic, to fail, once again, to take texts for what they are. Céline's subsequent volumes against the Jews and the concomitant course of European history have cast considerable doubt on the validity of Gide's conclusion, if not on his intention. Moreover, his own text stopped short of any discussion of what he claimed was the irreducible "Jewish problem," beyond the fact that—"God knows"—it existed and was—*contra* Maritain—essentially racial ("There is nothing to be done about that").[4]

The upshot of Gide's article, then, was that Céline's enemies, the wrongheaded defenders of the Jews, were quite simply deaf to his prose. *Tant pis!* Now that deafness to French, with its attendant impoverishment of French literature, was described in a page of Gide's *Journal* (24 January 1914) as *specifically* Jewish: "Why speak here of defects [*défauts*]? It is enough for me that the qualities of the Jewish race are not French qualities . . . the contribution of Jewish qualities to literature, in which nothing is of value that is not personal, brings fewer new elements, that is, an enrichment, than it cuts short the speech [*coupe la parole*], the slow explication of a race, and falsifies gravely, intolerably, its signification."[5] The burden of intolerance with which the final adverbs charge the paragraph is worth noting. For the page, whose pretext, ironically, is the literary criticism of Gide's friend and predecessor at *La Revue blanche*, Léon Blum, would regularly be trotted out by the French Right during the wave of anti-Semitism that greeted Blum and the Popular Front from 1936 through the Second World War.[6] Gide, despite his embarrassment, was explicit in refusing to disavow it.[7] A respect for style, in brief, would ground Gide's tolerance of Céline's anti-Semitic *opus*, even as it had offered a basis for his "intolerance" of Jewish literature.[8]

January 1914, the date of the entry in the *Journal*, is as well the date of publication, in the *N.R.F.*, of the first installment of Gide's satire [*sotie*], *Les Caves du Vatican*. It is tempting to speculate on the extent to which the observations quoted from the *Journal* constitute a context for Gide's *opus*, in what measure, that is, Gide's page of "anti-Semitism" is more than an aberration to be classified, regretted, and dismissed as such. What follows, then, is a discussion of *Les Caves* in terms of a series of intertexts it mobilizes, and their relation to what Gide, quoting Maritain, would call the "immense and painful question of the Jews."[9]

I

In broadest outline, *Les Caves du Vatican* is the story of the initiation, in spite of himself, of an elegant and sexy cosmopolite, Lafcadio, into a family of grotesques satirically representative of French society in 1893. The family—a precipitate, no doubt, of Gide's polemic with Barrès on the virtues of *déracinement*—consists of the spouses of three hapless daughters, each named after a flower, of a forlorn botanist.[10] The family (of brothers-in-law), that is, is structured as a plant, and the turning point of the novel will lie in Lafcadio's inadvertent grafting of himself into its tissue. The brothers-in-law are marionettes, joined less by any affinity of ideology than by their common mediocrity. We meet first Anthime Armand-Dubois, a sadistic positivist *savant*, author of anticlerical attacks in the Freemason press, who will undergo conversion to and from Catholicism by the end of the novel. The second is Julius de Baraglioul, a Catholic author of edifying—but barely readable—novels. The third is Amédée Fleurissoire, a devout Catholic merchant taken in by the diabolical and baroque swindle that gives the novel its name. Fleurissoire has fallen for a confidence man's line that the Pope has been secretly kidnapped by the Masons and replaced by an impostor. He sets off for Rome on a crusade to free the Pope from which he will never return.

Perhaps the most virtuoso strand in Gide's *tour de force* is dermatological. A full page is devoted to the sebaceous cyst [*loupe*] disfiguring Anthime's neck: "Here despite all my desire to relate only the essential, I cannot pass over in silence the cyst [*loupe*] of Anthime Armand-Dubois. For so long as I have not learned to disentangle more surely accident from necessity, what can I demand of my pen if not precision and rigor . . ." (p. 16).[11] There follows a paragraph on the emergence and growth of the excrescence, and the ensuing resentment and defiance of Divinity to which it drove its anticlerical bearer. Now in the course of the novel, Amédée Fleurissoire is afflicted with his own particularly nasty skin disorder, the inflamed pimples [*boutons*], resulting from insect attacks in cheap hotels on his way to Rome, that stud the nape of his neck. The condition reaches a head when Amédée visits a barbershop. The narrator indulges in one of his mock-lyric flights: "Oh somnolence, torpor of that tranquil little stall" (p. 157). By the end of the page, the barber, distracted, plunges Amédée into agony by inadvertently nicking one of the pimples ("*vlan!*") with his razor. It is as though the blemish on the nape of the neck were a family trait, the family held together less by blood than by the all too visible imperfections of its skin.

Enter Lafcadio, "at ease in his skin" [*bien dans sa peau*], aristocratically exuding well-being through every pore (p. 186). A different race? He is the bastard half-brother of Julius, the novelist, spawned by their father, Juste-Agénor, on a Rumanian courtesan during a diplomatic mission. Juste-Agénor, though formally disowning Lafcadio, simultaneously blesses him with an affection he can never marshal for his ludicrously pious scion, Julius. Julius, meanwhile, takes Lafcadio on as his secretary, and his single redeeming span in the novel comes in the brief stretch during which he giddily first anticipates, then recalls his thrill in conceiving of a totally unmotivated act . . . that Lafcadio, unknown to him, will have just committed. Julius: "profit is not always what spurs men to act . . . there are disinterested actions. . . . By *disinterested* I mean: gratuituous. And that evil, what is called: evil, can be as gratuitious as good, out of sheer overabundance and exuberance, a need for expenditure" (p. 179). Julius will eventually retreat from his conception of a gratuitous act into the Manichaean fantasmagoria that has motivated his brother-in-law Amédée. But Lafcadio, meanwhile, has attempted quite untheoretically to perform it, by kicking an aging and pathetic stranger to his death out of the train compartment they are sharing for the sheer pleasure the gratuitousness of the murder will afford him. The brothers-in-law calculate; he expends himself without forethought: a different race indeed. Yet no sooner is the murder consummated than it takes on the overdetermination of a dream-element. The stranger turns out to bear the ticket of Lafcadio's half-brother, Julius. For he is none other than Amédée, Julius's brother-in-law. He bears as well the cuff links [*boutons de manchette*] that Lafcadio had offered as a gift to his concubine. As Amédée goes careening out the train door, moreover, Lafcadio feels a terrible gash on the nape of his neck. Amédée has imparted the family mark—*loupe, bouton*—to Lafcadio, and by the end of the novel the adolescent hero will collapse, with diminishing enthusiasm, into the arms of Julius's beautiful daughter, Geneviève. The summit of indeterminancy and freedom, the gratuitous act, has turned out to *bind* Lafcadio into the family, to be in itself multiply bound or determined. The brothers-in-law, Lafcadio observes, were more intricately "ramified" than he suspected. He has been grafted onto their tree—a floral Oedipus, bearer of buds [*boutons*].

Two comments now, precisely on the button. First Gide, *Journal* (17 July 1914): "Wrote to Copeau, who is amazed that there is not more discussion of *Les Caves*: 'Why should I be surprised if there's no noise [*que ça ne sonne pas*]? I didn't press any button [*Je n'ai pressé aucun bouton*].'"[12] Then Proust, "captivated to the heavens and ravished by your *Caves du Vatican*," as he wrote to Gide in a dithyrambic letter of 6 March 1914. His enthusiasm knows but one (explicit) reservation: "There are certain things that I cannot bring myself to like in your *Caves du Vatican*. I am speaking not only of Fleurissoire's pimples [*boutons*], but of a thousand material details . . ."[13]

Let that distaste for Gide's *boutons*—which was to be the structuring trope of Lafcadio's entry into the family structure—serve to introduce the first of our intertexts, Proust's own novel. For it was only the previous year that Gide had rejected, with "extreme distaste," *Du côté de chez Swann* for publication by the *N.R.F.*[14] The Gide-Proust tension, that is, is at its most marked at the time of the observation on the Jews cited from the *Journal*, the time of *Les Caves*. Now at the node of Proust's volume—the famous goodnight kiss sequence, whose repercussions, the narrator writes, would never cease for him—Marcel finds himself desperate at finding his illicit wish to kiss his mother goodnight granted in a climate of extreme disappointment. His father takes off wearily to bed, his mother comes to his bedroom, and the decline of Marcel's will is sealed. I have demonstrated elsewhere the essential links between that "decline of will," emblem of life's evils, and the triumph of "involuntary memory," metonym of art's glories, in the *madeleine* episode.[15] In the present context, I would insist on the evocation of Marcel's father as he climbs the stairs on the night of the first sequence. He reaches the landing, "tall, in his white nightshirt . . . with the gesture of Abraham, in the engraving by Benozzo Gozzoli that M. Swann had given me, telling Sarah to leave Isaac's side."[16] The allusion, then, is to the binding of Isaac. With its motif of hostility between generations displaced in a symbolic sacrifice guaranteeing the future of the Jewish race, it may be thought of as a kind of circumcision, a decisive separation from the mother. Whence Abraham's gesture toward Sarah. Whence, as well, the irony of Proust's allusion, for *his* would-be Abraham abandons son and wife together and toddles off wearily to bed. Indeed, it may be demonstrated how elaborately the crucial figure of a failed circumcision structures the entirety of Proust's novel.[17]

Consider now Gide's ephebe on the occasion of his unwitting inscription into the family of *Les Caves*. Riding on the train from Naples to Rome, he savors his disgust at the unknown grotesque (Amédée) seated opposite him in their compartment: "Between that filthy creep and myself, could there be anything in common? . . ." (p. 189). Anticipation of the sheer pleasure of gratuitously victimizing the codger gives way to a childhood memory. During the first year he slept far from his mother, he was awakened once in the middle of the night by a surrogate father, one of his mother's lovers, Wladimir, "draped in a vast rust-colored caftan, his mustache drooping and his person capped with an extravagant night cap, erect like a Persian bonnet, which elongated him without end" (p. 190). Lafcadio's first thought is for his mother: sick? dead? Wladimir cuts short his attempt at questioning by placing finger to lips and gesturing to Lafcadio to rise. They take off silently, excitedly, as in a ritual, to a far corner of the house, where their silent escapade reaches its conclusion with the dipping of biscuits into two crystal glasses of Tokay from which they toast. "*Ni vu, ni connu*" (p. 192). Always already a dream. Whereupon Lafcadio awakes and excites himself to his gratuitious act, the murder of the pathetic stranger. Now in falling out of the train, Lafcadio's victim not only gashes the nape of his murderer's neck (*"griffe affreuse"*), as we noted, but seizes his hat: "and Fleurissoire found nothing else to grab on to than the beaver hat [*chapeau de castor*], which he seized desperately and took with him in his fall" (p. 196). The rest of the novel, as we observed, proceeds to undermine the freedom of Lafcadio's act, to bring him disdainfully into Geneviève's arms.

Gide, then, has given us the precise antithesis of the nodal configuration of Proust's novel of the previous year. A "father" performs the gesture of separation from the mother whose absence Proust's narrator regarded as the pivotal sadness of his life. Marcel's will would enter into decline, his life redeemable only by art: the explication of those experiences of involuntary memory emblematized by the *madeleine* dipped in tea. Lafcadio's dipping of biscuits, on the other hand, is inscribed as part of the ritual denied Proust. In *Du côté de chez Swann*, the nature of that ritual, the allusion to Abraham, led us to speak of a failed or absent circumcision. Recall now that Gide's dreamily phallic ephebe is projected into the cycle of familial (heterosexual) desire by an act that leaves him with the family mark on his neck, while removing violently his beaver hat. With the foreskin removed from the phallus, initiation, alas, has been achieved. A provisional formulation: whereas Proust's text of 1913 is balefully woven around a failed circumcision, Gide's *sotie* of the same year is an implicit lament on a fantasy of success in the performance of that ritual.[18]

A curious note of oblique confirmation may offer some clarification at this juncture. In the *Journal des Faux-monnayeurs*, Lafcadio would later surface as the prototype of the young hero (Bernard) of the only one of his fictions Gide himself called a "novel." Indeed the reference in that *Journal* to a "conspiracy taking place behind Lafcadio's back without his suspecting it" (6 July 1919) is close enough to Lafcadio's relation to the Vatican swindle in *Les Caves* to allow us to see in the *sotie* the prototype of *Les Faux-monnayeurs* itself.[19] Now in the *Journal* of the novel, Gide relates (5 March 1923) a dream of an evening with Proust during which he inexplicably cuts short a story Proust is telling by tugging at a string attached to two sumptuously bound volumes of Saint-Simon's *Mémoires* on the shelf. They come clattering down: "the boards were half torn from the back; the binding, in short, was in a lamentable state."[20] The attack on the volumes of Saint-Simon, an author central to Proust's novel, in many ways repeats the ironic assault on the *binding* episode of Proust's novel in *Les Caves*.

II

Let us then situate tentatively the fantasy of circumcision in *Les Caves* between the "anti-Semitic" page of the *Journal* in 1914 and the disparity, both figural and "ideological," with Proust, which did, after all, have as one result the rejection for publication of the beginning of Proust's novel. The flimsiness of that constellation, it will be objected, is manifest. For *Les Caves* is a satire of Catholic rather than Jewish France.[21] A single Jewish character, Eudoxe Lévichon, plays too insignificant a role in the work to sustain any modification of that judgment. Whence the interest of our second intertext (after Proust): Gide's play of 1896, *Saül*. The customary genealogy of *Les Caves* consists of tracing the bogus philosophical concept of a "gratuitous act" through the *soties*: *Paludes*, *Le Prométhée mal enchaîné*, *Les Caves*.[22] The results, however, are more surprising, though less "philosophical," I would suggest, if one views *Saül* as a prototext of *Les Caves*.

Gide's grim drama articulates the Biblical story of a difficult pass in the history of the Hebrew monarchy with a personal tragedy of pederasty unacknowledged. Saül, at the play's beginning, is plagued by demons, tyrannized by a wife he has never loved, depressed by the *fin-de-siècle* femininity of his son Jonathan. His army is meanwhile an easy prey to the Philistines. In his weariness, his one delight is David, the adolescent singer who entertains him, and whom he unconsciously, desperately, and unsuccessfully attempts to seduce. David's affection is entirely for Jonathan, and his great plan is to save Israel by taking command of the enemy Philistine army in order to bestow the crown Saül will in any event lose on his beloved Jonathan. Alas, in the course of his victory, Saül and Jonathan are both slain. David is condemned to continue the royal line of Israel.

Let us now flesh out the parallel with *Les Caves*. At the center of Gide's drama, we find Saül and his singer-harpist David. Gide would later use argot to describe his title figure (in a letter to Mauriac of 1 July 1922) as "an old king as pathetically ruined as a *cave*."[23] Saül, then, for all his suffering, is a dupe, laughingstock: *cave*. He is described at one point "as though an idiot" [*comme imbécile*] (p. 143).[24] David, on the other hand, is all toughness and grace. Saül: "What I love above all else in him is his strength. The suppleness of his loins is astonishing!" (p. 129). The relation between Saül and David, it may be intuited, is already that between Julius (dismissed as a fool [*cette andouille*]) and Lafcadio. King is to harpist as novelist is to secretary. This is confirmed by the precise homology between Samuel in the play and Julius's father, Juste-Agénor, in the *sotie*. Samuel, who had anointed Saül, has nothing but contempt for him. Rumor indeed has it that "before dying, the great Samuel went to Bethlehem, called little David close to him, and, in a small courtyard, seen by almost no one, took oil and anointed him—as he had done with Saül (p. 46). This reproduces the benediction Juste-Agénor secretly gives his bastard son just before dying: "Lafcadio, instead of throwing himself in the arms of the Count, kneeled piously before him, and, his head in his lap, sobbed, all tenderness in that embrace, felt his heart, with its fierce resolve, melt away" (p. 72). Lafcadio, it is clear, has replaced Julius in the affection of the classy cynic, even as Samuel was said to have secretly anointed David.

Consider now Lafcadio's "gratuitous act." A would-be disinterested act of aggression against one of the dupes [*caves*] results—mock tragically—in Lafcadio's integration into the family as recipient of Geneviève's affections. Without any of the philosophical speculation of *Les Caves*, David (of Bethlehem) takes up arms against Saül with total disinterest in order precisely to avoid succeeding Saül, to bestow the crown of Israel on Jonathan. David fails in his act of generosity even as Lafcadio had: each is drawn resentfully, gloriously, into the family. Once one collapses the three brothers-in-law of *Les Caves* into a single figure, both object of "gratuitous" aggression and would-be protector, the homology becomes clear. David takes the lead of the Philistines much as Lafcadio will attack Amédée. Each receives unwillingly a heritage as a result.

In *Les Faux-monnayeurs*, it may be noted, Edouard imagines an as yet inexistent literary genre: the Christian novel, as opposed to those novels of edification he despises. An example of a novel of edification is Julius's mediocre *L'Air des cimes*, which everyone in *Les Caves* finds unreadable. But is not David—of Bethlehem—already a hero of Edouard's other genre, his disinterested act and its failure a proto-Christian gesture in—and against—the kingdom of Israel? It is as though Lafcadio himself, repeating David's gesture, were paradoxically Gide's Christian hero, *Les Caves* a "Christian novel."

If the homology between Julius-Lafcadio-Juste-Agénor and Saül-David-Samuel, beyond any "philosophy" or "thematic" of the gratuitous act, is valid; if indeed Saül's demons, in their infernal playfulness, may be superimposed on the swarms of insects that attack Amédée on his way to Rome, a further superimposition may be affirmed between Geneviève (Julius's daughter) and Jonathan (Saül's effeminate son). Indeed Jonathan's death has as its counterpart the imaginary absence of Geneviève's phallus. The absence of the phallus, that is, marks the failure of the gratuitous act. Now it is remarkable that if one figure for the failure, the imperfection in Lafcadio's immaculate crime, is the loss of the beaver hat, the corresponding instance in *Saül* is David's unwilling reception of the crown of Israel. For that royal trapping is the play's principal prop, and David's perennial wish is "to get that crown away from me!" [*d'écarter de moi cette couronne*] (p. 132). It is as though our two texts found their ultimate point of articulation in a hat trick: Lafcadio's beaver cap spinning away and returning simultaneously as the crown of Israel.

That figure, we have posited in our reading of *Les Caves*, is one of circumcision. This should confirm for us the validity of our endeavor, since it is in circumcision, after all, that a problematic of anti-Semitism, to all appearances marginal in Gide, intersects with the question of sexual identity, one of his major concerns. The simultaneous removal and return of the hat, which marks our articulating instance, is perhaps a figure for a certain undecidability marking circumcision itself: metaphor of castration or feminization and of its opposite—defeminization through removal of that residual vagina, the foreskin.[25] Thus, in the anti-Semite's imagination, the typical Jew: servile (castrated) and arrogant (unduly defeminized).[26]

III

Two series, then, the French-satirical (*Les Caves*) and the Hebrew (*Saül*), as well as their capacity to absorb any reality (Lafcadio, David) beyond themselves, are articulated by our figure.[27] *La France . . . juive?* I would propose, after Proust and *Saül*, a third-intertext for *Les Caves*, the legacy of Edouard Drumont. For although Gide's sources for the Vatican swindle in the Catholic press of 1893 have been amply annotated, one wonders whether the rollicking futility of the *fin-de-siècle* wars between Catholic *bien-pensants* and Freemasons has ever been captured with more verve than by Bernanos in his life of Drumont, *La Grande Peur des bien-pensants*.[28] In his chapter "Le Nonce du Pape et le bienheureux Léo Taxil," the author evokes the career of Léo Taxil, Drumont's enemy and a notorious swindler. From which:

> A magnificent story! A certain number of good people, whom nothing will ever fatigue, terrifically well-intentioned, to the point that on the model of Juvenal's courtesan—to quote his savage phrase—no cheese will ever make them vomit, still take seriously, forty years later, one or two episodes of a fraud that was nevertheless as simple, as summary as many a celebrated swindle. A former seminarian, half pornographer, half blackmailer, supplier of specialized bookstores, then a bookdealer himself, founder of an "Anti-clerical Bookshop" in which he published allegedly popular pamphlets, a veritable banquet for the obsessed, had suddenly announced his return to God, promising at the same time to the devout bullfrogs, through imminent revelation of the secrets of Freemasonry, to which he had adhered, an abundant ration of muck. Thousands of simpletons, male and female, were immediately burning to learn, from the mouth of the prodigal son, the famous secret rites, suspecting in them, no doubt, several details of wondrous obscenity, terror and torment of their anxious chastity. The Anticlerical Bookshop, from one day to the next, became the Antimasonic Bookshop, tripling or quadrupling its clientele. . . . This prodigious mystery ended as abruptly as it had begun: with a pirouette. To the terror of the good canons, threatened with apoplexy, the neophyte, inundated with benedictions, as stuffed with pious confections as the parrot of the good ladies of Nevers, calmly stuck his tongue out at his new audience and declared that he had treated himself to a good laugh at the expense of his mitered hosts—and that he was, moreover, more of a Mason than ever, having turned over to the curiosity of the *bien-pensants* only the most obvious of secrets. . . . The alleged revelations, confessions, pages that had caused so many tears to flow were a crude fabrication written—by our sharpster—on the marble top of a café table slimy with syrup and absinthe. Still more: even during the period of his greatest fervor—an unheard of touch—the favorite of the pious public had not foregone the profits of the Anticlerical Bookshop. In plain sight of his dupes, he had left its administration to Mme Léo Taxil, who faithfully contributed, every month, to the common till innumerable free-thinking pieces of a hundred *sous* each, fraternally mixed with clerical coins of like denomination, gathered elsewhere . . . .[29]

Taxil, then, was extorting a profit from the conflict between Catholics and Freemasons, ready to change sides as business demanded. (This, of course, is much the structure of the swindle in *Les Caves*.) Now it happens that the single cause he engaged in without deception was apparently the opposition to Drumont's election to municipal office on an anti-Semitic platform—i.e., the defense of the Jews. *La Grande Peur des bien-pensants*, it should be noted, is not an attack on the Jews so much as on those too timid to embrace a doctrine as radical as anti-Semitism. Here again we approach *Les Caves*. For in 1892, the year prior to the action of Gide's *sotie*, Taxil, after his conversion, published *Pie IX Franc-Maçon?*[30] That volume was an effort to discredit (several times over) a Freemason legend that Pius IX had been a Mason early in life, and that the Pope consequently, in excommunicating the Masons, had excommunicated himself. As the Palermo Lodge put it: "The malediction and excommunication thus fall on his own head; he is, moreover, in consequence of that very act, guilty of perjury. The Pope is thus excommunicated by himself."[31] Taxil's book is painstaking in its refutation, offers 50,000 francs on its cover to anyone able to discredit any of its arguments, and even goes so far as to reproduce alleged photographs of the Pope in Mason attire in order to discredit them in detail. Consider then that his apparent effort consists in cutting short a "schism" within the Papacy (the self-excommunication of Pius IX) by thwarting a fraudulent attempt by Freemasonry (through rumor) to seize the Pope, to turn him into a Freemason. But the effort, we recall from Bernanos, was only apparent; it was in fact part of Taxil's larger swindle. With this spurious "attempt" in 1892 to prevent a Mason discrediting of the Church through "seizure" of the Pope, his "replacement" by a Freemason, we have reproduced, above and beyond any newspaper articles Gide may have consulted, the configuration structuring the swindle in *Les Caves*.

Now 1892 was as well the year of publication of Drumont's *Testament d'un antisémite*.[32] The first chapter, "Paroles testamentaires," has as its epigraph a letter of indignation from the author to a friend. From which: "I have seen the Papal *nuncio*, Rotelli, kiss Léo Taxil, the author of *Amours secrètes de Pie IX*, on the mouth. Following the example of my divine Master, Jesus, I had taken the defense of the oppressed against the robbers and exploiters of the poor . . ."[33] The final chapter is called "Léo Taxil et le nonce du pape." It deals with Taxil's (successful) opposition to Drumont in the municipal elections of 1890, but above all with the author's shock that contemporary Catholicism—in the person of the Pope's own representative—had fallen so low as to embrace the likes of Taxil. For such is the world in which "our French Catholics," in all purity of conscience, "arrive in Rome replete with their illusions and all the candor of a simple soul. They are instructed to lay down their satchel of Peter's pence, that the alms—precious before God—of so many poor believers have swollen, and, when that is done, the entire Roman community, clerical, or anticlerical, black or white, bursts out laughing in their faces."[34] All roads, decidedly, seem to lead to the Rome of Gide's *Caves*.

Now to attack Drumont in 1890 was inevitably to defend the Jews. And Taxil did.[35] Conversely, to attack Taxil, for Drumont, meant to lash out at the Jews. Thus, from his *Testament*: "I have had the curiosity to survey the unspeakable work of this man, at present so dear to our ecclesiastical authorities. Understandably, the first publishers of his books had been Jews: Strauss in Paris, Millaud in Marseille. It is truly a descent into the Jewish Inferno, that excremental Hell described by Swedenborg, the 'polluted Jerusalem, emitting a stench of rats, and across which Jews, bespattered up to the spine, run through the muck in pursuit of a few coins of gold.'"[36] The power of Taxil, that is, is that of *la France juive*. And the ire of Drumont finds its target at the end of *Le Testament d'un antisémite* in the Vatican itself: "'He has no political sense, this Frenchman,' [the Papal *nuncio*] will perhaps murmur upon reading me; 'he hasn't understood the *combinazione*. Léo Taxil gets on well with his Excellency *moussu* le baron de Rothschild, and *moussu* le baron de Rothschild is very good indeed; he's already arranged a few deals for me.'"[37] It is perhaps in this context that the character of Eudoxe Lévichon in *Les Caves* may be situated. His last name, we read, is an agglutination of Lévy and Cohen, his first Greek for *bien-pensant*. It will be recalled that his is the slightly unscrupulous intelligence behind the business in cardboard religious statuary in which his partner is Amédée. The initial investment of capital in *Le Carton Romain plastique* is 60,000 francs, precisely the sum first extorted in the Vatican swindle. The Jewish reference is close at hand.

Midway, then, between Drumont's attack on Taxil, the conclusion of his *Testament* (1892), and Bernanos's effort to receive that legacy (of anti-Semitism) in *La Grande Peur des bien-pensants* (1931), we find, in the year of Gide's pronouncement against "Jewish literature," *Les Caves du Vatican* (1914). I am suggesting less a "source" for Gide than a tradition of discourse that is particularly "enriching"—in the sense that Jewish literature was imagined as impoverishing—for the comprehension of his text. As though the Drumont-Bernanos nexus, after Proust and Gide's own *Saül*, offered a matrix of intertexts which quite simply fulfilled the criteria of a more satisfying reading of *Les Caves*. It is perhaps in this context that "accusations" of anti-Semitic (authorial) intent, as the New Critics might say, sadly reveal their ultimate irrelevance.[38]

IV

Beyond the Taxil chapter in *La Grande Peur*, *Les Caves du Vatican* and its world, of course, know something of a future in Gide's own fiction. Specifically, Lafcadio is present in *Le Journal des Faux-monnayeurs*, as we saw, as the prototype of Bernard. And beyond that, Lafcadio-Bernard, we learn from the *Journal*, was slated to make an appearance in Gide's unfinished *Geneviève*.[39] Lafcadio-(Bernard)-Geneviève? Such was, of course, the tentative couple formed at the end of *Les Caves*. The eventuality that Gide's fictional career should run amuck in the effort to reimagine that coupling in his *Confidence inachevée*, as *Geneviève* (1936) was subtitled, will occupy us shortly. In preparation for that discussion, we shall first turn briefly to *Les Faux-monnayeurs*.

At what is perhaps the pivotal moment in Gide's contrapuntal novel, Alfred Jarry makes a cameo appearance at a literary banquet and provokes general chaos by firing—gratuitously?—a blank shot. In the ensuing confusion, Gide reshuffles the cards of his novelistic deck: Olivier links up with Edouard, and Bernard, formerly Lafcadio, is dragged under the table by Sarah. His heterosexual initiation—with Sarah—will take place that night: "Bernard has hardly slept. But he has tasted, that night, a forgetting more restful than sleep; at once an exaltation and annihilation of his being. He glides into a new day, a stranger to himself . . ."[40] One thinks of the end of *Les Caves*, the act of love initiated by another random act of violence: "Love drives her [Geneviève], impels her toward him. Lafcadio takes her, presses her, covers her pale forehead with kisses. . . . We leave our two lovers at the hour of the cock's crow, when color, warmth, and life at last triumph over the night. Lafcadio, above the sleeping Geneviève, rises . . ." (p. 249). The ambivalent initiations to heterosexual love, the dawns, and the prior acts of random violence as well confirm our impression. For the presence of Jarry joins up with the scholarly tradition associating the figure of Lafcadio with Apollinaire.[41] The elements of that tradition are numerous: Apollinaire's notoriety as perpetrator of an absurd criminal act (his alleged theft of the *Mona Lisa* in 1911), his illegitimacy, his contempt for print, his middle-European adventuress-mother, the legend that his father was chamberlain to the Pope . . . The details need not concern us.[42] In the present context, the usefulness of finding a figure of Apollinaire (in *Les Caves*) in something like the position of Jarry (in *Les Faux-monnayeurs*) is in confirming the relations between the meetings of Lafcadio and Geneviève in the earlier work and of Bernard and Sarah in the later one.

Consider now *Geneviève*, the unfinished conclusion to the triptych that began with *L'Ecole des femmes*. Gide's *Journal* entry of 9 March 1930 reads: *Geneviève* or *La Nouvelle Ecole des femmes*—in which I shall deal directly with the whole question of feminism."[43] Gide's pained comments in the *Journal* about his inability to complete the work convincingly are ultimately confessions of just how alien a "feminist" position was to his art.[44] There is a telling irony in the lines the pseudo-narrator addresses to the author-publisher of her account: "You see how far we've come, M. Gide, from the considerations that dictate your books."[45]

Now if the *Journal* recounts Gide's retreat from *Geneviève*, *Geneviève* recounts, in its strongest passages, a related retreat. The first section of the book deals with the constitution of a protofeminist league by Geneviève and two *lycéenne* comrades. The group, in fact, crystallizes around the figure of Sara, a Jewess whose charismatic charm is much evoked in terms of her brash Orientalism.[46] Geneviève's attraction to the exotic Jewess deepens to a point of crisis. That pivotal moment comes with the public reproduction of a painting by Sara's father, in which she may be seen lying nude, her face hidden by the mirror she appears to be peering into. The scandal in Geneviève's family is such that they withdrew the permission they had accorded her to frequent Sara.

Geneviève's reaction is, first, a surprising agreement with her unloved father: "What caused me the most suffering was not being able sincerely to rebel against my father's judgment, feeling—in spite of myself—scandalized at the idea that Sara could have exposed herself like that, let herself be seen without clothes, and in front of her father."[47] Simultaneous with her own retreat from Sara is a growing awareness of how eroticized her relation to the Jewess had become:

"An unknown anxiety convulsed my face [*me décomposait*]. I did not realize it was desire because I didn't think one could experience desire for anyone but a being of the other sex."[48] Her separation from Sara is consecrated by a period of illness and convalescence. The second part of *Geneviève* waxes feminist-ideological, seems devoid of sentiment. The concluding section 3, unwritten, would seem to relate the circumstances by which she finally manages to have a baby, a project that had been cold-bloodedly and unsuccessfully pursued in the previous section (2). Painter believes that the child's father would have been Bernard of *Les Faux-monnayeurs*.[49]

The retreat from the novel, then, was at some level a backing away from the desire of the Jewess (Sara), itself inseparable from the "question" of feminism. In *Les Faux-monnayeurs*, we observed Bernard-Lafcadio enter into an affair with a (Protestant) Sarah who has much in common with the Jewess of *Geneviève*.[50] In that later work, Geneviève's desire is fixated on Sara. Her ultimate coupling—with Bernard —is thus doubly mediated by Sara(h). And it is that coupling that Gide could not bring himself to write. When we recall the trickiness of "circumcision" in (and out of) *Les Caves du Vatican*, its role in the final mating of Lafcadio and Geneviève, we are tempted to speculate that the unspeakable *desire of the Jewess*, in all senses of that phrase, always already lay at the virtual core of the *sotie* of 1914 as well.

At this distance in abstraction from the passage on "Jewish literature" in the *Journal* that served as our point of departure, the path back to that pre-text proves surprisingly sure. Consider that the occasion of Gide's attack had been his irritation at the drama criticism of Léon Blum. Now the work of Blum's that most annoyed Gide, according to the *Journal*, was *Du mariage*, which he was inclined to regard as a "skillful preface to the whole of Jewish theater today."[51] Blum, in fact, suggests that the argument of his book is contained in a speech by the heroine of Porto-Riche's play, *Amoureuse*.[52] The thesis of his book is that the institution of marriage can be saved, the ravages of prostitution eliminated, only by granting women a measure of premarital sexual freedom comparable to that enjoyed by men. In a marginal notation, he had written: "The whole of my reform: tolerate, organize the freedom of girls before marriage."[53] His tract, then, was neither socialist, nor particularly Jewish, but feminist: self-consciously devoted to the sexual emancipation of the women of the French *bourgeoisie*.[54] For Gide, however, its insistence on female pleasure was specifically Jewish. The fourth dialogue of *Corydon*, his apology for and celebration of pederasty, in fact, offers itself as a refutation of *Du mariage*. Corydon's interlocutor, admittedly a foil for Gide's protagonist, waxes vehemently anti-Jewish.[55] Corydon, though never quite rallying to the anti-Semitic line he is offered, is intent on finding a solution other than Blum's to the specific problem of prostitution. His answer is self-consciously *un-* (if not *anti-*)Jewish: recourse to the Greek institution of pederasty as an outlet for the surplus of male sexual energy in nature. As for female sexual pleasure, we are told that it is irrelevant: "Girls in Greece were raised with an eye not so much to love as to maternity."[56] Whereupon the antipathy to the Jewish feminist, Sara, in *Geneviève*, its role as a figure of Gide's own inability to complete that work, again reveals its coherence.

Further confirmation of the links between antifeminism and anti-Semitism comes in an odd page that Gide wrote, but which remained unpublished until after his death.[57] It features, once again, Gide's quintessential Jew, Léon Blum, and recounts what he called his own favorite Jewish joke [*ma plus belle histoire juive*]. The humor of the story lies in the following circumstance: In July 1900, Gide, in need of a lawyer, contacts his friend Blum, who recommends a fellow Jew of unsavory demeanor named Fischer. Gide pays Fischer, but gets no satisfactory results. His patience considerably strained, Gide makes several inquiries and discovers that Fischer has done nothing for him. Several days later, he learns that his lawyer has just been reprimanded on another matter by the French equivalent of the bar. He tells Blum, expecting his friend to be beside himself with shock, but is told instead: "The wretch! he's started in again."[58] The punchline establishes, with mild humor, that contrary to expectation, corruption is the norm, rather than the exception, for Blum and his crowd. Now the interest of the story, I believe, lies not where Gide pretended, but rather in the legal case the author wanted to press: the collection of damages from an insurance company for an accident his wife had incurred. Here, then, is the first paragraph of Gide's "joke": "In July of 1900 (I can easily find the date), as we were leaving for the country, my wife managed, with a single stroke, to have her two arms crushed [*trouva moyen de se faire écraser tout d'un coup les deux bras*]. It was while crossing the Place de la Concorde; she was in an uncovered vehicle; another car happened to brush against hers. Seeing the person in the other car rise, my wife, seized with fear, stood up as well without taking the precaution of holding on to anything. The two cars banged in to each other, and there was Madeleine thrown onto the pavement. Before she had time to recover, a heavy truck that was passing, its driver looking elsewhere, crushed her two arms, which were stretched in front of her. Had she not instinctively raised her head a bit, she would have been done for. . . . But it is not the accident that I want to talk about. . . ."[59] The upshot of the passage is that an elaborate recounting of the humiliation and mutilation of his wife was not, in Gide's discourse, a matter grave enough to inhibit the success of a joke which, one feels, was sufficiently feeble to have a hard time withstanding the slightest obstacle to its effectiveness. And *that* fact suggests that the aggression of Gide's humor was directed as much against his wife as against the Jew. But Blum's intellectual stance at the time was oriented primarily toward the sexual emancipation of women. So that the joint targets— Jew and woman—of Gide's story are inextricably intertwined.

In his *Portrait d'un Juif* (1962), Albert Memmi quotes Gide, again on Léon Blum: "I was horrified by his way of approaching me when I met him by chance in a theater corridor after years of silence, his way of putting his arms around my neck and asking me: 'How is Madeleine?'"[60] For the reader of Blum's militant analysis of female sexual satisfaction in chapter 2 of *Du mariage*, the question, coming from Blum, was no doubt embarrassing. For the author of *Si le grain ne meurt* and *Et nunc manet in te*, it could provoke only "horror." As for the gesture of arm (or hand) on neck, we are hard put not to recall Amédée Fleurissoire's aggression against Lafcadio . . . in the course of his murder. As the strands—of anti-Semitism and antifeminism—proliferate and converge, one is tempted to attribute to Gide's quotation of Blum's query on Madeleine a role, in its virtuality, as central to his work as that played by the inquiries into the status of a different *madeleine* in the novel of his half-Jewish rival and friend, Proust.[61]

V

L'aigle battit des ailes,
roucoula. D'un geste atroce
Prométhée ouvrit son gilet
et tendit son foie douloureux
à l'oiseau.

—Gide, *Le Prométhée mal enchaîné*

Lest "Jewish literature" cut short his word [*"qu'elle ne coupe la parole"*] . . . thus ran the anxiety of the *Journal* entry of 1914. Having observed a fantasy of circumcision flower—or bud—in *Les Caves*, the desire of a Jewess convulse—or "decompose"—Geneviève, indeed the composition of *Geneviève* itself run aground in the process, we sense how paradoxically, metaphorically close Gide came to something of a rudimentary program for an entire wing of his own fictional edifice in that entry. *Geneviève*, part 3 remains unwritten; the program—necessarily—incomplete. It would remain for others to execute that relation to incompletion, to carry to its limit as prose the object of his anxiety. In conclusion, then, several remarks on that accomplishment.

Perhaps the greatest heir to Gide's *Caves* is Genet's *Notre-Dame des Fleurs*, a baroque celebration of the gloriously "immaculate" murder by a homsexual stud of a toothless old man: "the killer . . . rises, erect as a god, suddenly, on an altar . . ."[62] The murder of his pathetic victim transforms the phallic killer, inscribes him into the parody-religion of flowers: "if he knows . . . that his destiny is being accomplished at every instant, he has the pure mystical sentiment that his murder will make of him, baptized in blood: Our Lady of the Flowers . . . Killer [*assassin*]. He does not say the word to himself, but inside his head I listen along with him to the peal of a carillon which must be composed of all the bellflowers [*clochettes*] of lily of the valley, the bellflowers of spring, of porcelain, glass, water, air . . ."[63] Thus does Genet exacerbate and celebrate what in Gide had activated all the resources of the novelist's irony. At the other end of his ordeal, having all but ejaculated his confession ("it was rising, rising"), Notre-Dame says at his trial the words that will ensure his decapitation.[64] The Presiding Judge: "What do you have to say in your defense?" Notre-Dame: "The old guy was finished. Couldn't even get a hard-on [*Y pouvait seument pu bander*]."[65] The exchange, transcribed back into the measured terms of Gide's text: (Julius): "What was it you had against Fleurissoire, that worthy man of so many virtues?" (Lafcadio:) "I don't know. . . . He didn't seem happy . . ." (p. 242). The parallel is clear. Lafcadio, as we saw, had been the proto-Christian David of Bethlehem in *Saül*. In Genet's passage to the limit, he will figure as Jesus himself: "as prodigiously resplendent as the body of Christ rising—to remain there alone, permanent—in the sun-drenched sky of noon."[66]

Jewish literature? *Notre-Dame des Fleurs* is one of those works in relation to which something of a history of contemporary French thought could perhaps be written. It is, however, not my intention in this context to discuss the successive hold on its text exercised by Sartre's *Saint Genet* and Derrida's *Glas*. I would insist rather on the extent to which Derrida, in moving beyond a dialectics of consciousness (Sartre), beyond a dualistic problematic of "castration" (Freud), has turned his work into a protracted meditation on the institution of circumcision. In one column Hegel, and the lessons to be culled from the homology: woman to man, Jew to Christian, plant to animal, sign to sense. The Jew-woman-flower cut short—of meaning—at the stem. In the other, Genet, and the baroque construct of a floral Oedipus [*anthoedipe*], to use a term that already found its place in our reading of Gide.[67] Now in one of those extended insertions in the second column in which textual commentary offers itself as "self-analysis," Derrida quotes a passage from *Notre-Dame des Fleurs* on erotic tatoos: "Thousands of minute strokes of a fine needle marking the skin down to the blood, and the most extravagant figures are displayed for you in the least expected places. When the rabbi slowly unrolls the Torah, a mystery grips the entire surface of the skin with trembling, as when a colonist [*colon*] is seen undressing."[68] The male body as Torah. Derrida inserts the "inscribed column," the Torah to be wrapped, into an observation on circumcision (which Mauss had analyzed as a form of tatoo) and the bands in which babies are bundled after that ritual is performed. But the allusion to Torah in Genet gives way, in *Glas*, to a childhood memory of a synagogue in Algeria: a child—the author, "himself"—assisting in the unwrapping of the glyphic scroll, the spreading of the disrobed body of the Torah, the men following each other up to the sacred scroll, as in an orgy. The inscribed phallus—through what prodigy of subincision?—opens up into the body of an Oedipal mother. And all the while the prayer shawls of the men, wrapped around their necks like unknotted ties, reveal that we are being treated to a Jewish rewriting of Notre-Dame's immaculately conceived murder ("Je suis l'Immaculée Conception") of his toothless victim, a rewriting itself of the not so gratuitous act we have thematized as Lafcadio's circumcision. Derrida observes that a child present at such a ceremonial reading of the Torah can perhaps find therein the wherewithal to order all the fragments of his life. Then: "What am I doing here? Let us say that I am working at the origin of literature, by miming it."[69] It is one "origin" of that "origin," somewhere between Gide's *Journal* and his *sotie* of 1914, that this essay has attempted to chart.

CONCLUSION

> . . . entering into the opponent's strength
> in order to destroy him from within . . .
>
> —Walter Benjamin, quoting Hegel,
> *Schriften*, vol. 2, p. 481.

> Quotations in my works are like robbers
> by the roadside who make an armed attack and
> relieve an idler of his convictions.
>
> —Walter Benjamin, *Schriften*, vol. 1, p. 571.

Each of the four essays in this volume grew out of the enigma posed by a fragment barely assimilable by the authorial *corpus* of which it nevertheless forms part: Blanchot's contributions to *Combat*, Lacan's allusion to *Le salut par les juifs*, Giraudoux's anti-Jewish diatribe in *Pleins pouvoirs*, Gide's page against "Jewish literature" in the *Journal*. Were I to summarize my effort in each case, it would be to construct a logic of each author's work that would restore the fragment to a position at the core of each *oeuvre*. In the course of each excursus, moreover, matters were pressed to the point of a reversal (in values) figurable by the rhetorical device of chiasmus. Our first essay delineated a shift within the posterity of Bernanos from an anti-Semitic configuration to an identically structured philo-Semitic one. Our reading of Lacan with Bloy charted an inversion of Freud's experience upon visiting the Jewish ghetto of Hamburg. Giraudoux's *La Folle de Chaillot* was read as a reverse-return of Racine's *Athalie*. Finally, we noted the crucial shift in values—from Proust to Gide—attributed to a fantasy of circumcision.

CONCLUSION

Now the valorization—and repercussion—within the works studied of the shock elicited by each of those fragments has led, I believe, to an enhancement of our historical understanding, indeed of our literary pleasure. This in turn brings us to the crucial question of the status of a historical understanding or literary pleasure generated through what must be admitted to be the construction—or, worse yet, the restoration—of a lost anti-Semitic tradition. In the introduction to these essays, I invoked Freud's radical articulation of interpretation, masochism, and repetition, and commented that in matters of textual analysis, we are hard put to move beyond *Beyond the Pleasure Principle*. The present volume, however, may allow us to follow a quite different track from Freud's in an effort to see how far it will take us, how primary, in fact, masochism in analysis may or may not be.

Before we pursue that path, a word situating this effort within contemporary criticism may be in order. For despite the heterodox focus on anti-Semitism in France, these essays are in their moves, I believe, of a piece with the general interpretative effort called "deconstruction." The discovery and valorization of the marginal, that is, and its intricate displacement to a strategic (near-)center from which a chiasmic shift in the values of a *corpus* may be effected strike me as among the most difficult and rewarding gestures that reading at present allows.[1] A discussion of the structure of my endeavor, then, may shed some light on "deconstruction" in general. For the fragments I have chosen to "valorize" for analysis, in addition to being marginal, are taboo. Anti-Semitism, by dint of Europe's recent history, is one of the few taboo regions of speculation in our secularized democracies. Here then lies a margin one can pretend to displace only at some risk . . . For it is one thing to attempt to perform a Nietzschean dance, another to do so, in Gershom Scholem's phrase, in the devil's own arms.[2]

It is Gershom Scholem's complex rehabilitation of the Sabbatian movement in his 1937 essay, "Redemption through Sin," that will serve as my point of departure. Scholem's fascination with Sabbatai Sevi is part of his effort to restore to Jewish Messianic thinking that element of apocalyptical discontinuity which nineteenth-century rationalism, with its investment in the idea of historical progress, had repressed.[3] For the catastrophe marking the advent of Sabbatai Sevi as would-be Messiah in the seventeenth century was ultimately that he was, to all appearances, a fake. Sabbatai Sevi, in Scholem's version, was a "psychotic" declared by his therapist-illuminate, Nathan of Gaza, to be the Messiah.[4] The mobilization of the Jews of Europe around his calling was massive and intense. But the movement was to know its greatest challenge and originality in 1666 when the alleged Messiah, under threat of death, converted to Islam. For Sabbatianism became thereupon the anomalous effort to accommodate the paradox of an apostate Messiah. Apostasy, after all, was an even more disturbing fate for a Messiah than crucifixion, and the reserves of Jewish interpretative agility needed to save this Messiah for Judaism would be great indeed.

It is at this juncture that we approach the subject of this book. For the solution of the Sabbatians was to see as the Messiah's ultimate task a plunging into evil in order to defeat it from within. It is as though the movement of restorative synthesis (*Tikkun*)—whereby redemption, in the old (Lurianic) Kabbalistic mode, would be effected—were to be deferred. The Messiah must dwell in those dark, hylic forces, the *Kelipoth*, consign his holiness into that fallen state which the Kabbalists called the "breaking of the vessels" [*shevirat ha-kelim*].[5] Now in its more radical formulations, Sabbatianism called on its followers to emulate the Messiah, commit (apparent) apostasy, and most generally abide by the antinomian precept that the fulfillment of the law lay in its violation: "*mitzvah ha-ba'ah ba-averah*"—literally "a commandment which is fulfilled by means of a transgression."[6] As the Jew drives himself deeper into (holy) sin, Jewish life becomes a celebration of the radical discontinuity between outward sign and inner sense, perhaps of the arbitrary nature of the sign *per se*. Finally the entire movement would come to grief in the late eighteenth century in the Sabbatian group in Poland headed by Jacob Frank, "the most hideous and uncanny figure in the whole history of Jewish Messianism."[7] Frank schooled his followers in the arts of ethical and sexual transgression, eventually led his flock to Catholicism, all the while declaring this "apostasy" part of the divine scheme of things. In Scholem's terms, "for the Jew who saw in Frankism the solution to his personal problems and queries, the world of Judaism had been utterly dashed to pieces . . ."[8]

It is one of the originalities of Scholem's analysis to see the Jewish Enlightenment less as following the lure of rationalism away from the faith than as being the precipitate of that savage exacerbation of a transgressive faith—Sabbatianism—once its justifications were no longer felt. The mystically inspired transgression of the Law, that is, was the condition of the Enlightenment's possibility and not its radical opposite.

The cataclysmic side of Sabbatianism, moreover, was to result in remarkable sympathy with the French Revolution when it came. The heir apparent to Jacob Frank in the sect of Offenbach was sent to the guillotine with Danton in 1794.[9] Scholem's story ends with the arrest of the followers of Frank in 1799 after the circulation of their "Red Epistle."[10] For the references to Jacob (Frank) in that mystical document had misled the police into suspecting criminal allusions to the Jacobins. The matter was eventually cleared up, and the Jews were released, but it was not until Scholem's essay that the profound justification of the arrest of the Frankists as Jacobin sympathizers was understood.

Scholem's essay ends, that is, at the point of inception of our subject in these pages. For the opening lines of Drumont's *La France juive* are: "Taine wrote *La Conquête jacobine*. I intend to write *La Conquête juive*."[11] Thus begins the *opus classicus* of anti-Semitism in France. But Scholem's essay has a more essential link to our effort, since it offers a model of what these pages have attempted: as though our construction of a logic of anti-Semitism were, in Scholem's terms, a latter-day version of that quintessential Jewish heresy of plunging into the hylos of the *Kelipoth*, writing *as* the breaking of vessels.

* * *

Scholem's investigation of seventeenth-century Jewish Messianism and its posterity was, in fact, part of one of the great intellectual ventures of the twentieth century: his own ongoing debate and friendship with Walter Benjamin.[12] For it is enough to read the references to Messianism in Benjamin's *Theses on the Philosophy of History* to sense how parallel his own efforts to break with the progressivist ethos of social democracy were with Scholem's attempt to discredit, say, Heinrich Graetz's historicist-continualist interpretation of the Messianic idea.[13] Scholem's return to the "false Messiah" is of a piece with Benjamin's celebration of the "*weak* Messianic power" with which every generation is endowed.[14] It is the pertinence of that *weak* Messianism to interpretation in general that I have aimed at in evoking the anachronistic case of Scholem's Sabbatai Sevi in this conclusion.

Scholem himself has discussed Benjamin's relation to Messianism in a memoir of their friendship entitled "Walter Benjamin and His Angel."[15] The angel is a painting by Klee (*Angelus Novus*) that hung, at different times, in both their houses, and served as something of a talisman of their friendship. Scholem first discusses two versions of a text by Benjamin dealing with an angel and entitled enigmatically "Agesilaus Santander." In that piece, the narrator says he was given by his parents at birth two additional non-Jewish names should he ever become a writer and need to "demonstrate" that he were not Jewish. Yet he keeps these names secret, and compares them to the secret Hebrew names Jews give to their children. The name, by analogy, is both Hebrew and non-Jewish, and by the end of the text, in Scholem's privileged reading, it will become by way of anagram *The Angel Satan* (*Der Angelus Satanas*). The angel-name, moreover, figures a kind of essential impoverishment of language ("in no way is this name an enrichment of the one it names . . ."), the temporal-spatial medium of what Derrida would later call *différance*: "I came into the world under the sign of Saturn—the star of the slowest revolution, the planet of detours and delays."[16] It is an angel that will not deliver his message. In one of the *Theses on the Philosophy of History*—that bears an epigraph by Scholem and is something of a postscript to "Agesilaus Santander"—the Angel is borne helplessly backward into the future, observing impotently the catastrophes of history pile up before him.[17] The Angel, that is, *is* a failed Messiah, delayed, in an essential way, midst the breaking of vessels.[18]

Scholem reminds us that his Messianic figure, curiously enough, is a precipitate of French literature: "The Luciferian element, however, entered Benjamin's meditations on Klee's picture not directly from the Jewish tradition, but rather from the occupation with Baudelaire that fascinated him for so many years."[19] Toward the end of his life, Benjamin was in fact considering relinquishing the Baudelaire project in favor of a study of the history of "sincerity" from Rousseau to Gide. He thus wrote (in French) to Gretel Adorno (17 January 1940): "I have not settled the basic question: whether I would do better to lay the grounds for the comparative study of Rousseau and Gide or rather undertake without delay the remainder of the *Baudelaire*."[20] By 7 May, he had opted for the *Baudelaire*. Nevertheless, Gide was clearly a major focus for Benjamin, a sometime literary correspondent charged with reporting on French letters. Consider now, in the context of the secretly Hebrew, non-Jewish angel-name, the following fragment from a letter of Benjamin's to Ernst Schoen (19 September 1919): "I admire in Gide a marvelous and serious agitation; [*La Porte étroite*] contains 'movement [*Bewegung*]' in the highest sense of the word, as few books do, almost like *The Idiot*. Its Jewish seriousness [*sein jüdischer Ernst*] corresponds to my own feelings. And yet the whole of the work seems broken, as light in a cloudy liquid, caught in the subject matter of a narrowly Christian-ascetic sequence in the foreground," a fundamentally "lifeless" medium.[21] The quintessential contemporary French author, then, Gide, seems secretly Jewish in his "movement," but hidden—like light in cloudy waters—within a Christian frame. Twenty years later, having interviewed Gide for the German press, written extensively about him, Benjamin quotes and comments on the following sentence from a text we have already encountered, Gide's "Les Juifs, Céline et Maritain": "If one were to see in *Bagatelles pour un massacre* anything but a jest, Céline, despite all his genius, would be inexcusable for stirring commonplace passions [*remuer les passions banales*] with such cynicism and off-hand frivolity."[22] Benjamin, 16 April 1938, comments in his letter to Horkheimer: "Le mot 'banal' en dit long. I too, you will recall, had been struck by Céline's lack of seriousness [*Mangel an Ernst*]. Gide, moreover, moralist that he is, is concerned solely with the intention—and not the consequences—of the book. Or has he, Satanist that he is, nothing to object to them?"[23] Here the hidden presence is Gide secretly—Satanically—seconding Céline's anti-Semitic fun. The hidden Jew of the 1919 letter, that is, here corresponds to the crypto-anti-Semite. In the earlier letter, on *La porte étroite*, we had Jewish seriousness, movement [*Bewegung*] immobilized in a Christian frame. In 1938, we find at the surface Céline's lack of seriousness and, more secretly, Gide's hypothesized identification with Céline's achievement in stirring—or "moving" [*remuer*]—the passions of anti-Semitism. In "Agesilaus Santander," the secret name—both Hebrew and non-Jewish—of the Angel was Satan, a bequest, wrote Scholem, from Baudelaire.[24] In the case of the quintessential French contemporary, Gide, the adjective "Satanic" is used to describe that hidden Hebrew—non-Jewish (anti-Semitic) movement. To write about Gide with the "weak Messianism" that is the endowment of the interpreter in the second *Thesis* meant at some level to *affirm* the fantasy of the *Angelus Novus*, watching impotently a single "catastrope which keeps piling wreckage upon wreckage and hurls it in front of his feet."[25] And to do so, in 1938, as a Jew. The earlier letter on Gide, we noted, had as its occasion a reading of *La porte étroite*. The last line of the final *Thesis*, the end of Benjamin's oeuvre, reads: "Every second of time (for the Jews) was the strait gate through which the Messiah might enter."[26]

Thus, then, did Benjamin find in "French literature" an exemplary medium through which to plunge—with weak Messianism—into the catastrophe about to engulf the Jews. For if indeed the measure of the Messianic idea in Judaism, as Scholem claims, is a life lived in deferment, there can be little doubt that in the economy of the friendship between Benjamin and Scholem, the quintessential deferment was the trip to Paris rather than Jerusalem. Both friends were aware of the significance of Benjamin's choice to announce a delay in his journey to Palestine in a letter written to Scholem (20 January 1930) in French: *"auf Französisch!"* as Scholem writes.[27] It is in fact tempting to trace in the correspondence between the two friends the stages along the ultimately suicidal path that the Parisian detour—"'Pariser Passagen': theater of all my struggles and all my ideas"—was to figure for Benjamin.[28] From his letter of 4 March 1939 to Scholem: "It happens that of all the different danger zones in which the world is at present divided for Jews, for me France is the most threatening, since here I am *completely* isolated economically [*weil ich hier ökonomisch voll-kommen isoliert stehe*]."[29] Scholem recounts Benjamin's failed efforts to gain French citizenship under the hoped-for aegis of Giraudoux and Gide.[30] As the situation worsened, the compulsion to affirm his links to French literature became increasingly desperate. In 1939, the year Jouhandeau, in *Le Péril juif*, swore to denounce all Jews to "the obloquy of my people," Benjamin may be found pleading that he was the first German to recognize the importance of the author of *Prudence Hautechaume*.[31] Thus Benjamin's path of humiliation, ending in the suicide and burial in an unmarked grave in what one is tempted to imagine as the anti-*cimetière marin* of Port Bou.[32] It is as though, within the friendship, Benjamin's planned "journey to Palestine via France," a voyage squandered in its primordial detour, were a motif harmonic with that of "redemption through sin" in Scholem's study of the legacy of the Sabbatians.[33] To which we return, for it is within that harmonic that the essays in this book have been written.

* * *

It is important to insist on the break within Kabbalist Messianism that the Sabbatians represented. The Lurianic school of Safed in the sixteenth century presented a cosmic myth of exile and redemption. God created the world in order to rid himself of evil. The history of the world is the gradual process of restoring divinity—and the world—to itself. It would indeed be possible to view Luria's Kabbalah as a classic of traditional hermeneutics, interpreting ever closer to the Origin under the tutelage, no doubt, of a strong—messianic?—master.[34] Sabbatianism, on the other hand, the last historical conflagration of the Messianic idea in Judaism, is a Messianism gone astray on its way to redemptive meaning. In its radical form, it accommodates the apostasy of the Messiah by making of the Jew's life, as we have seen, a desperate celebration of the arbitrariness of the sign, a performance of its fundamental discontinuity in relation to inner sense.[35] It is to be a better Jew that the Sabbatian must break the law of the Torah, a law perpetuated as its own transgression. *"Bittulah shel torah zehu kiyyumah,"* as Scholem quotes the rabbis: "the violation of the Torah is now its true fulfillment."[36]

The emblem of that common investment in "weak" or "false" Messianism that joined Benjamin and Scholem, we have seen, was Klee's painting, *Angelus Novus*. Scholem informs us that before fleeing Paris to the Spanish border, Benjamin freed the Angel from its frame and stuffed it into one of two suitcases which Georges Bataille had agreed to hide for him during the war in the Bibliothèque nationale.[37] For the German Francophile had been an assiduous presence at the Collège de Sociologie.[38] Bataille, summarizing his argument in *L'Erotisme*: "Transgression is not the negation of a prohibition [*interdit*], but its completion and transcendence."[39] Thus, I suspect, would run a neo-French gloss on the Hebrew concept *mitzvah ha-ba'ah ba-averah* ("a commandment which is fulfilled by means of a transgression") that Scholem has labored (against the rabbinical tradition) to rehabilitate.[40] Somewhere in between the two, the apocalyptics of Benjamin and his Angel.

For a number of years now, French thought—in its "poststructuralist" phase—has lived lavishly out of the conceptual baggage of Bataille. Perhaps the ultimate horizon of the essays in this volume lies in seizing the emblematic value of that relic of a joint fascination with a Messianism gone astray: the Klee Angel, stashed away in the suitcase in Bataille's keep. As though a certain genealogy remained only to be freed from Bataille's custody to reveal its transformative effects. It is toward a delineation of that possibility that I have attempted to write.

APPENDIXES

The following essay on writing as a "breaking of vessels" deals with the works of Julien Gracq. I have included it not because of any relation of Gracq's prose to anti-Semitism (I know of none), but because of its intersection at several junctures with concerns developed in the conclusion to this book.

APPENDIX I. BLACK GRACQ[1]

Jack, Now *arch*. M.E. (a. F. *jaque* in
OF. also *jaques*, Ult. origin uncertain.)
. . . A vessel for liquor; orig. of
waxed leather coated outside with tar
or pitch (−BLACK JACK 1)

Jack, . . . A ship's flag of smaller
size than the ensign, used at sea as a
signal, or as a mark of distinction;
spec. the small flag, indicating nationality,
which is flown from the jack-staff at the
bow of a vessel.

−O. E. D.

Why Julien Gracq? This reading of an author whose principal works, written in the forties and fifties, are perhaps too uncomfortably recent to warrant rediscovery, was born of my surprise upon encountering Gracq, in the first volume of his *Lettrines*, on Jules Vallès.[2] Perhaps a word on the circumstances of that surprise will serve to situate the pages that follow. I had recently completed a reading of Marx's classical texts on the (failed) revolutions in France of 1848 and 1871.[3] In both cases, the key to Marx's achievement, I suggested, lay in the laughter attendant on a certain break with dialectics: the Bonapartist short-circuit of the struggle between bourgeoisie and proletariat after 1848; the Communard break with the comedy of complicity staged by Prussian "master" (Bismarck) and Third Republican "slave" (Thiers) in 1871. The paradox of finding the Commune (of 1871), within the

logic of Marx's writings, structurally homologous to the Bonapartist co-
hort (of 1851) was sufficiently strange as to allow of resolution only
within what I termed (evasively?) a fantasmatics of history. For the
Bonapartists, it should be recalled, figure in Marx's argument as the
"antithesis" of the Commune, and in his rhetoric, at the end of a memorable paragraph from *The Eighteenth Brumaire of Louis Bonaparte,*
as "the whole amorphous disintegrated mass of flotsom and jetsom the
French call *la bohême*."[4] It was at this juncture that Gracq—on Vallès
—reserved his surprise. For his *lettrine* is a meditation on a single sentence of *L'Insurgé*, in which the (Communard) narrator comments
that his first book had its inception in the stir that Murger's burial
had aroused in him. Gracq: "Bohemians of the pen, freelance journalists, grizzled teaching assistants, aging students, half-diplomaed and
in search of a paying pupil: it is indeed the small world of the *Scènes
de la vie de Bohême*, turned to vinegar, which bestowed on Victor Noir
so handsome a funeral and governed with incompetence the Commune
midst the pipes, pints, *glorias*, smoke, and shoptalk of the editorial
room of a 'small newspaper.'"[5] There ensues Gracq's reaction of "nausea" upon following in Vallès's text the "ubesque mess" into which the
Commune degenerated under such leadership. It is a page as striking in
its "savage gaiety" as any of those of Marx to which Gracq attributes
that grace in an earlier *lettrine*.[6] But, virtuosity aside, the brief meditation on Vallès—as "Chaplinesque *pétroleur*"—and the Bohemian Commune offered *as history* a remarkable coincidence with the coherence
in Marx's text I had hesitated to qualify as other than *fantasmatic*. This
struck me as sufficient reason to undertake the fullscale reading of
Gracq that follows. That a certain structure of unreality at the core
of history figures as the horizon of Gracq's novelistic *oeuvre* is perhaps ground for regarding the inception of these remarks as less personal than may be feared.

I

On two occasions, in his *Lettrines*, Julien Gracq, writing of Mallarmé,
imagines him as having written in the wrong language. First, German:
"one would have preferred it to be written in a more hierarchical language, one more mindful of the external signs of respect—like the
splendid German language in which every noun explodes in majesty
behind its capital."[7] Then, Latin. Reference is made to a "syntax of

Latinate type": "Constantly, subterraneanly magnetized by the absolute ablative, infinitive proposition, verbal noun, apposition, constantly
threatened with embolism, Mallarmé's prose advances through a series
of minute blockages, from which it is extricated by as many perceptible
jolts."[8] Germanic to the point of explosion, then; and Latinate to the
point of embolism. If we bracket the question of the accuracy of
Gracq's two-part fantasia on Mallarmé for a moment, we find it as-
suming an oddly familiar coherence. For French *embolie*, the diction-
aries remind us, from the Greek *embolê*, means the sudden obliteration of a vessel by a foreign body. An incursion into foreign—German,
Latinate—waters accompanied by a devastating—explosive—attack on
a vessel. Somewhere between international politics and the physiology
of circulation, Gracq has served up the central fantasy around whose
absence his major novel, *Le Rivage des Syrtes*, was written. For *Lettrines*, in an attack against formalist criticism's inability to gauge the
role of the unwritten "fantom books" around whose suppression many
a text is "completed," has occasion to refer to Gracq's novel of 1951:
"*Le Rivage des Syrtes*, up to the final chapter, progressed canonically
toward a naval battle that was never waged."[9] The speculations on
Mallarmé always already translated—from the German, from the Latin
—are thus secretly organized around the very sequence—naval catastrophe or the obliteration of a vessel—whose virtuality oriented the
writing of Gracq's most elaborate novel.

What is elided metonymy in *Le Rivage des Syrtes* is metaphor in
Un Beau ténébreux. That novel's subject is the (near-)rush to destruction of a seaside group of vacationers—known as "la bande *straight*"—
in the wake of a suspiciously charismatic desperado, Allan. The narrator meditates on the amphitheater constituted by the lodgings along
the curving beach: "Benches of a Colosseum ranged around some
naumachia [*quelque naumachie*]." The image is no sooner proffered
that it opens a precipice within the text: "I suddenly find in that banal
remark something—I can't tell what—erratic and exalting." By the end
of the paragraph, that naval battle—the almost ocular focus of the
novel's drama, but the point of convergence [*moyeu*] as well of the
spokes of a wheel about to take off—has given way to a sacrificial flame
in which life itself is consumed in a spasm of intensity: "that a single
flame in which life in its supreme tension is resolved might purify and
deliver with a gasp ten thousand hearts."[10]

Now, Gracq's first novel, *Au Chateau d'Argol*, offers a moment homologous to the one we have just observed in *Un Beau ténébreux*. For that work is presented as a demonically anti-Nietzschean recasting of Wagner's *Parsifal*. Another vessel, then, the Grail, incarnate this time in the woman Heide ("In a second, Heide peopled the room, the castle, and the entire country of Argol with her radiant and absorbant beauty").[11] Albert and Herminien, versions of Perceval and the Fisher King, join in savaging the vessel: "the stares of Albert and Herminien, attracted in spite of themselves by the focus of that luminous enchantment [*féerie*], crossed in a flash and understood each other."[12] As in *Un Beau ténébreux*, communion is established in a contemplation (productive) of flame. The double focus is devastating: "to plunge her into the heart of their double life, and scorch her with the fire of that light unknown to men."[13] But the devastation is imaginable, in this Gothic Parsifal, as the obliteration of a vessel: "She became an immobile column of blood . . . it seemed to her that her veins were incapable of containing another instant the frightening flow of that blood . . . and that it was about to gush out and spatter the trees with its hot jet."[14] Parsifal, classically, pits the Grail against an incomparable wound. Gracq, in his black reading, would offer a vessel imaginable as a wound exploding with blood. Vessel (Grail) versus vessel (vein): what *Un Beau ténébreux* calls *naumachie*. Or the same vessel always already split — in meaning — cracked, or better, *gracqued*. Around which, at an already appreciable distance from Surrealism's *vases communicants*, is established the bond — or *bande* — of what *Au Chateau d'Argol* sings as the brotherhood of men: "*la fraternité virile*."

A vessel divided against what one has difficulty calling itself. In *Les Eaux étroites*, an evocation of the small but exquisite pleasures of a familiar excursion on the River Evre, a landscape in which virtually nothing has changed over the years, an invitation to dream immutability, a single change does, nevertheless, stand out: "The last time I saw the wash-boat [*bateau-lavoir*] of la Guérinière, many years ago already, it had sunk, while listing [*en donnant de la bande*], but only up to half the length of the small columns supporting its canopy, a bit in the inglorious posture of the Vichy fleet, scuttled at Toulon in the shallows: it seems that a whole fantasy of youth had nosed its way, without stir, into the mud along with it."[15] By the text's end, the (fantasied) shipwreck (of fantasy) is assumed to be final. Once again, then, however differently, following Gracq's associations, the privileged — virtual — object is the vessel divided against itself

(Vichy scuttling its own fleet) and giving—us—in its obliqueness: *de la bande*.

Return to *Le Rivage des Syrtes*, or rather to a curious speculation, in the second volume of *Lettrines*, on its genesis. The novel is centered on Aldo's fascination with the line of demarcation separating the waters of his native Orsenna from those of Farghestan, with which Orsenna has been in a state of lapsed—or dormant—war for three hundred years. To cross the Line dividing that Dead Sea is to press beyond the nihilism of his decadent land, at the risk of rekindling the war, that is, of total destruction. The maritime poetry of the text is organized around the fantasy of setting out from one's coast, risking everything in a crossing of the Line at sea. Now in *Lettrines*, Gracq recalls his residence from 1942 to 1944 at Caen, during which time he was tantalized by the interdiction under which the Germans had placed the coast. "Perhaps the patrol line, in my novel, which cuts across the Sea of Syrtes is ultimately daughter to that line of demarcation—less well known than the other and, moreover, barely guarded—which for two years bolted shut all access I might have to the band along the coast [*la bande côtière*]."[16] "La bande côtière," "la bande straight"—and its rush to destruction in the wake of a Christlike desperado—I have suggested, is the subject of Gracq's first novel after the war, *Un Beau ténébreux*. So that access to it would appear to lie at a highly charged juncture between history and Gracq's text. Indeed, the *Lettrines* anchor the *bande côtière* in the history of the novel as well. By the end of the fragment just cited, Gracq finds himself correcting a misimpression of having taken the rickety train along the coast on his first trip to the sea after the war. "After the fact [*après coup*]," he writes, he had obviously supplemented his failing memory with a recollection from Proust's Balbec.[17] Later in the volume, Gracq, rereading *Sodome et Gomorrhe*, sees in the coastal train the specific *medium* of the pleasures the novel affords: "a comedy of manners—rendered freer and more airy by the swimming season—was played out along that strip of a dozen stations it caused to vibrate from one end to the other and exist as sonatina does a keyboard."[18] Whereupon a series of personal recollections leads him to reflect that the childhood pleasures of a ritual train ride to—or by—the sea were such as to grant the fixed litany of stations, "in the gradation of progressively fulfilled expectations, a solemnity hardly inferior for childhood to what might obtain, in the gradation of anxiety, for that of the stations of the cross."[19] From the line—or band—along the coast to the itinerary of Christ, the allusions to Proust offer a re-markable transition between the poetics of *Le Rivage des Syrtes* and those of *Un Beau ténébreux*.

But consider the strangeness of the *bande* in the earlier *lettrine*. It is constituted by a doubling inland, i.e., *within*, of the line whose whole force lay in its access to or delineation of otherness, exteriority. The impossible trip *from* one's coast was then always already doubled by a prior impossibility of reaching one's coast. Whereupon the entire thematic of the launching of a ship, around which attempts have been made to organize Gracq's writing, is unsettled.[20] For the paradoxical specificity of the *bande côtière*—the matrix out of which Gracq's novels may be generated—is to figure a periphery within.

Whereby we again approach the question of translation: a crucial stretch (or band) of German within French as well as its germinality for the novels. As though the notion of a French ideally always already translated from the German in Mallarmé were in fact more properly applied to Gracq himself. Mallarmé, of course, never felt more French than when confronted with Wagner. "Richard Wagner" is indeed the title of a text subtitled "Rêverie d'un poète français."[21] Gracq, on the other hand, seems never more quintessentially himself than in those oblique homages to Wagner which, for example, precede *Au Chateau d'Argol* (a demonic rendering of *Parsifal*), *Le Roi pêcheur* (a theatrical treatment of the same material), or *Un Balcon en forêt* (whose epigraph is from act 1 of *Parsifal*). Himself? Julien Gracq was in fact the pen name taken by Louis Poirier in 1938 upon publishing *Au Chateau d'Argol*. Its protagonist was named *Al*bert. In 1945, *Un Beau ténébreux* centered on *Al*lan; *Le Rivage des Syrtes*, in 1951, on *Al*do. The onomastic system into which Gracq has written himself—GRAcq-AL—returns us to the split in the vessel. Gracq marks the crack in the GRAAL (Grail), the opacity of fiction to authorial consciousness (Gracq is above all split off from Albert, Allan, Aldo . . .). As though the world itself were the hemorrhage, dividing author from work, of Mallarmé's embolism in the earlier *lettrine*.[22]

German, but also, ideally, always already translated from the Latin, suggested Gracq, concerning Mallarmé. The year 1938, when Poirier took on his pen name, was the year Giraudoux undertook *Les Gracques*.[23] The Latinate resonance of the name was blatant. Now whatever other interpretations recourse in 1938 to the crises initiated by the Gracchi may be available to, those crises were initiated by and centered upon an attack against the category of representation.[24] Whence we approach the implicit politics of the split in Gracq's Graal. The Germano-Latinate Mallarmé of *Lettrines* figures a ruse dealt out in the game of blackgracq.

II

In 1958, Gracq published *Un Balcon en forêt*, his last novel and, in more senses than one, a culmination of his novelistic endeavors.[25] *Au Chateau d'Argol*, published in 1938, his first novel, had aspired to being a Gothic version of *Parsifal*. The 1958 work takes up the Parsifal mythology and situates it in 1939-40, the period of the *drôle de guerre*. Full circle, or almost. At the same time, André Breton's anointed heir — describing himself as "fundamentally allergic to realism" — found himself writing what he calls a realist novel: "Reality furnished too much, it was moving too far in my own direction."[26] The coincidence of Gracq's privileged fantasmatic with a historical sequence — for such is the substance of what he calls *réalisme* — was bound to take its toll, and it is to the effects of that contact, a virtual conflagration within the myth, that I would like at present to turn.

The epigraph of *Un Balcon en forêt* consists of the opening lines of Wagner's *Parsifal*: ("He! ho! Waldhüter ihr/ Schlafhüter mitsammen/ So wacht doch mindest am Morgen").[27] The Waste Land here is Third Republican France. The knights of Montsalvage are soldier-watchmen along the Meuse, near the Belgian border, in an isolated *blockhaus*, during the *drôle de guerre* ("prowlers of the confines, idlers of the apocalypse . . .").[28] May turns out to be the cruelest month, and indeed the novel's accomplishment as prose may lie in its evocation of the shattering (or nauseating) noise of the invasion: the "sheets of throbbing engines" [*nappes de vrombissements*] and "uninterrupted panting of motors" that obliterate the silence of the forest.[29] Grange, the protagonist of the novel, lieutenant in charge of the *blockhaus*, is seriously wounded in the thigh — "his leg was growing black" — in an escape from the fortification. He goes off to sleep, perhaps to die, in the home of his mistress, Mona, who has joined the exodus to the West.[30] Grange, then, is a kind of Amfortas — the Fisher King — stranded in the debacle: Grange: neither Albert, nor Allan, nor Aldo, nor indeed Perceval but a mollified Gracq, softened at its extremity beyond any aspiration to the *Graal*—in terms not simply military, *réserviste*. Gracq's last novel ends: "Then he drew the cover up over his head and went to sleep."[31]

Now in 1948, in *Le Roi pêcheur*, Gracq had already curtailed the Wagnerian plot. The play ends with Perceval's silence, his refusal to ask the question that would both heal and relegate to ordinary humanity the maimed King. Whence the despair of Kundry—*die Heidin* (Wagner), Heide (in *Au Chateau d'Argol*)—whose whole effort has been to risk annihilation in her seconding of Perceval's calling. "I await the conqueror," as she puts it.[32] But the conqueror comes only to be persuaded—or frightened—out of his mission by Amfortas. Parsifal, that is, does not ask the question: "What name is yours, more resplendent than wonder?"[33] Amfortas, in his nihilism, has won the day, but the preface of the play, curiously, concludes with the observation that in the general redistribution of values in the myth performed by the author "it is Kundry who bears my colors."[34]

Kundry: "I await the conqueror." Transposed to *Parsifal* 1958 (*Un Balcon*)—i.e., 1939–40—the logic of that fidelity to Kundry would have Gracq wishing for, yet writing against, the arrival of the Germans. Against: for even as Perceval in 1948 is devastatingly silent at the crucial juncture, in the later text he is present as sheer noise, a conflagration in the myth: "an enormous buzzing [*bourdonnement*] . . . one thought at first of a strange meteoric phenomenon, an aurora borealis in which sound would inexplicably have been substituted for light."[35] As though the myth itself were being devastated, consumed by its coincidence with history. Whereafter, Gracq ceases to write novels.

"Visibly something was being mimicked here, but what?"[36] That question, posed at a crucial juncture of *Un Balcon en forêt*, finds one answer in—or as—*Le Rivage des Syrtes*. Again, we are confronted with a *drôle de guerre*, in a state of dormancy but awaiting to be awakened. Substitute France for decadent Orsenna, Germany for barbaric Farghestan, and Belgium for *la mer des Syrtes*. Now Vanessa, in the earlier novel, finds herself in a position structurally identical to Kundry's and offers a virtually Nietzschean transposition of Kundry's "I await the conqueror": "beyond the blind and imbecile excitement straining in the endless night of its petty ambitions, there is room, should one not be afraid of feeling extremely alone, for an almost divine bliss—in passing *as well* to the other side, experiencing simultaneously the force and the resistance. Those whom Orsenna in the naiveté of its heart (which is not always that naive) calls thoughtlessly deserters and traitors, I have occasionally called, for myself, poets of the event.''[37] The poetic effect is one of polemical difference, gauging beyond any synthesis, the liberating potential of the clash *per se*. Vanessa, then, like Kundry in 1948, presumably bespeaks the poet's will to write, simultaneously, from without, from beyond the Line limiting the familiar, in alliance with the devastation with which foreignness itself threatens.

Now in *Un Balcon en forêt*, Vanessa's divine *jouissance* has its analogue in a fantasy indulged by Grange soon after the initial German invasion has swept beyond the *blockhaus*. He feels strangely, giddily drawn toward the frontier: "How far could one continue walking like that? he thought in a stupor, and it seemed to him that his eyes were pressing against their sockets until they hurt: there had to be *defects*, unknown veins in the world into which it were enough to slip a single time . . . 'I may be on *the other side*,' he thought with a tremor of sheer well-being; he had never felt in such intimacy with himself.''[38] That progress is cut short by a contingent event; but the (italicized) point of breakage as—or in—a vein, the as yet unknown "jubiliation" in anticipation of "cutting the moorings one by one," assure us that we are in proximity of the cracked—or gracqued—vessel and the host of germinal associations we have seen it command. As though Grange, at this juncture, were revealed to be a contraction of that invitation to expenditure *par excellence* in Gracq, the open sea: *le grand large*.

III

During the war, Gracq seems to have known a moment comparable in its intensity to his fantasy, in the novel(s), of passing *to the other side*.[39] For such is the impression the author gives in a recollection of his accidental discovery, in a station at Angers, of Henri Thomas's translation of Ernst Jünger's *Auf den Marmorklippen: "Les Falaises de marbre* left me in front of the station gate, in Hemingway's words, 'as empty, changed, and saddened as any exalted emotion.'''[40] The reference to Jünger in Gracq's criticism is recurrent, and, indeed, "La Littérature à l'estomac" has Gracq giving "almost all of the littérature of the last ten years for the single and barely known book by Ernst Jünger, *Auf den Marmorklippen*.''[41] Jünger's capriccio, for such was his characterization of his work, relates the reminiscences of an aged botanist-herborist, formerly a warrior, who has retired with his brother to a hermitage, where he pursues his inquiries, at the edge of the marble cliffs of a mythical country. What he recalls is the destruction of the idyllic life he and the entirety of the mythic land led as they gradually fall prey to the machinations of a cynical *Oberförster* (*Grand Forestier*, in the French) and the bands he mobilized in his totalitarian takeover of the society.

Jünger's novel was published in September 1939, the date when the action of *Un Balcon en forêt*, the *drôle de guerre*, begins. Indeed, the link between the two novels, the convergence between the myth the one seems to negotiate and the history of the other would reinvent, is more profound. For the idyll in Gracq's *blockhaus* — at Hautes Falizes — before it is shattered by the arrival of the German armies, is informed by the same metaphoric scheme as that orienting the botanists-herborists of Jünger's hermitage, on their *falaises*. Whence Gracq on his novel: "When you say that nothing happens in *Un Balcon en forêt*, you are right. Nothing or almost nothing, except at the end when, all the same, the war does break out. But for me something transpires which is quite important, something which produces a surface: the flow of time . . . and of the seasons . . . I feel myself by affinity to be not of the city, but a rustic, and I have risked the word *plant* to define man . . ."[42] Where Jünger presents two herborists in their hideaway, Gracq, through his soldiers in theirs, would join the tradition of those writers — such as Tolstoy — he terms "les grands végétatifs . . ."[43] Thus, as well, from *Lettrines*, vol. 2: "As the years have passed and I have progressed in my books, it seems to me that my vision has changed somewhat . . . and that the human figures that circulate through my novels have gradually become *transparents* — with a minimal index of refraction — whose movement is registered by the eye, but through whom it never stops perceiving the backdrop of foliage, greenery, or sea against which they move without ever quite detaching themselves."[44] The totalitarian onslaught, the idyllic life of male friendship, but above all the nexus of man and/as plant thus lead us as well toward Jünger when Gracq in his 1938 version of *Parsifal* returns to observe "that the war, even in its detail, was mimicking something, without our being able to know exactly what."[45]

Gracq himself is eloquent on the specific fascination of Jünger's work: "I believe that *Auf den Marmorklippen* must be read as a book of emblems. There are great images traversing it which have been, which are still, those of our life as men of the middle of the century, our joys and disasters, but they are to be found therein only as Alexander the Great, for example, may be discerned beneath the emblematic image of the King of Clubs: they have become the figures of a bizarre game, a great game [*grand jeu*]—simplified, captured as in a contour of eternity, and which nevertheless—simply to touch them—burn anew the fingers of the player. . . . They are the figures of our *hand* [*donne*]: moving or terrifying, they are the figures in which our destiny has been distributed to us."[46] Literature at its most intense, then, as a card game—potentially, I would suggest, *blackgracq*. For the science of heraldry or emblems, central to an understanding of Jünger, works as well for Julien Gracq-Louis Poirier the transition between the poetic effect *per se* and the author's signature or name. From *Les Eaux étroites*: "My mind is so made that it is without resistance before those random aggregates, adhesive precipitates that the shock of a preferred image anarchically condenses around itself. . . . Such fixed constellations (the emblematic links which old families, from their beginnings, established between name, arms, colors, and motto would not fail to cast light on their origin), however arbitrary they may at first appear, play for the imagination the role of singular transformers of poetic energy . . ."[47] Poetry thus has an essential relation to onomastics, an intuition we shared first in our delineation of the novels oriented around a split, crack, or gracq in the vessel of the Graal, and, then again, upon consideration of the speech act on whose absence the most explicit of Gracq's versions of *Parsifal*, *Le Roi Pêcheur*, concludes: Parsifal's (non)utterance of the question: "What name is yours, more resplendent than wonder?" It is within the virtuality of that question that the following comments on *Auf den Marmorklippen* are offered.

Jünger himself came to his title long after he had begun writing the book. Two months into the novel, he observed, in *Strahlungen*: "*The Queen of Serpents*—I may perhaps come upon a better title, lest we be taken for Ophites," a gnostic sect of "brethren of the serpent."[48] The core of the "beauty, grandeur, and danger" the book would convey, then, is perhaps in the elaborate episodes concerning serpents. Chapter 3, for instance, evokes the profound complicity the herborists of the hermitage enjoy with the snakes that inhabit the cliffs. From which: "Finally, when the white gravel of the serpents' path flared up in its furnace, the fer-de-lance vipers came slithering, slowly, and soon covered it as a mummy's wrapping [*bandelette*, in the French] is covered with hieroglyphics."[49] The amiability of the serpents is ensured by the ritual of their feeding. They are given milk from a silver basin to which they swarm. Erion, natural son of the narrator, moreover, is able to elicit the ludic potential of the serpents by striking the basin—as a bell—with a wooden spoon. *Fer de lance*/sustaining basin: one suspects that Gracq, in this sequence that gave Jünger's capriccio its initial title, intuited the figures of his own hand or *donne*—lance and Grail, for the Grail, in the iconography, was as often a dish as a chalice. But beyond myth (*Parsifal*), Jünger was perhaps dealing—Gracq—a very different hand. For the vipers reappear toward the end of Jünger's book in far more threatening guise. The circumstance is the invasion of the hermitage by the *lumpen* crowd of the *Oberförster* along with its pack of killer dogs: "The somber pack [*bande*, in the French], drunk with joy, invaded the enclosure in which our lilies were growing."[50] Whereupon the basin (of milk), the substitute breast (*toc-sein*), reemerges as an alarm bell (*tocsin*).[51] "The child seized the silver basin, which had remained in the courtyard after the serpents' meal. He struck it, no longer, as was customary, with his spoon of pearwood [*cuiller de bois de poirier*], but with an iron fork. He awakened in the basin a sound similar to a peal of laughter, well made to chill men and beasts. I perceived a rustle in the anfractuosities at the foot of the marble cliffs, then the air filled with a subtle and manifold hissing. Flashes of light glimmered across the bluish garden, and the brilliant vipers shot out of their crevices." The description continues: "they slowly rose to a man's height. And at that altitude, their heads oscillated like a heavy pendulum; their teeth, ready to attack, gleamed fatally, similar to styluses of curved glass [*wie Sonden aus gekrümmtem Glase*]." The queen of serpents—the Gryphon—then wraps herself around the leader of the pack of dogs: "then the Gryphon seemed barely to graze him near the ear [*ganz leicht am Ohr zu streifen*], and shaken with the convulsions of death, the dog rolled in the bed of lilies, lacerating his tongue with his fangs [*die Zunge sich zerbeissend*]." Such is the signal for the troop of serpents to attack its prey, whom they enlace "so tightly that a single body, covered with scales, seemed to envelop men and dogs. And it could be said that a single cry of agony shot out of that tight-knit complex [*diesem prallen Netz; ce réseau serré*, in the French], which the force of the venom, like an invisible noose, immediately strangled." From *toc-sein* (false breast) to *tocsin* (alarm), and from tocsin (alarm) to toxin (venom) as well. But what if we were to imagine the hand dealt to Julien Gracq né Louis Poirer by Jünger—or his translator—in this sequence? The clapper of a bell, a tool (made) of *poirier*, is replaced by a metal utensil, and then, ultimately, by the oscillations of a serpent head (*telle un lourd pendule*), to end at the teeth—a stylus of glass. But the serpents were always already figured, in their sinuosity, as the hieroglyphs on an Egyptian wrapping sheet or *bandelette*; indeed both the syntax of the French (*comme une bandelette se couvre*) and the narrative (of enlacement) suggest that the serpents are both the writing and the surface written upon. The queen of serpents passes her stylus of glass by the ear of a dog, who dies lacerating his own tongue. Whereupon the signal is given for the *bandelettes*—of glyphs—to enlace the *sombre bande* to the point of indistinction and death.

In metonymy, then: a process that begins with the oscillations of a utensil of *poirier* ends with the devastating reinscription of a *bande*. But the *bande* (*côtière*), we saw, in its germinal potential in the novels of the former Poirier, was always already the result of a reinscription within of the line fixing the limits of France, or perhaps French, ultimately from German. To cross that limit—which limit?—in (the novel of Jünger in) the novels of Gracq is perhaps to intuit a new resonance in the aesthetic of the "human plant" toward which the essays of *Préférences* tend, to broach a new complexity in Parsifal's unasked question: "What name is yours . . . ?" It is the conditions of that question's focal unutterability in the writing of Julien Gracq, midst the displacements and reinscriptions (*bandelettes*) of the process of reinscription itself, somewhere between history and literature, France and Germany, that these remarks have attempted to sketch.[52]

IV

ils n'eurent, malgré toutes les apparences, d'autre but que d'effectuer une mutuelle *reconnaissance*, de reconstituer et de se faire toucher l'un à l'autre avec un plaisir aigu la ligne de démarcation infiniment sinueuse que le choc de ces deux êtres, tant de fois renouvelé, avait fixé dès longtemps dans l'espace idéal où ils se réfugiaient.

Au Chateau d'Argol

Uber die Linie. In a celebrated essay on (and letter to) Ernst Jünger, Heidegger chose to reinscribe Jünger's title, to move from a "topography *trans lineam"* [*über die Linie*] to a "topology *de linea"* [*über 'die Linie'*].[53] In the German, in the Latin, in terms, moreover, that could be extrapolated into a general economy—or hymenographics—of the poetry of Mallarmé . . .[54] Heidegger's deconstruction (he uses the word) lies within his affirmation of the oscillation between the two identical titles, the affirmation that "the going beyond nihilism requires that one enter into its essence, which entrance vitiates the will to go beyond." Perhaps our reading of the geographer (topographer) Gracq with Jünger has repeated Heidegger's gesture: "topologized" the reinscription of a line of demarcation to the point of evacuating thematics itself.[55] In Heidegger's terms: "Is the human substance already in the passage *trans lineam*, or is it only entering the vast region which precedes it?" In our own: the central Gracquian theme of the launching of the ship is unsettled by our discovery that the line beyond which that process must press is displaced from inland: from within. As though the *bande côtière* were the "vast region" evoked by Heidegger.[56] The philosopher wonders what language is spoken by the thought whose fundamental effort is to cross the Line. And yet his reading of Jünger is universalist or planetary in perspective. In 1939, he writes, *The Marble Cliffs* were being read in a horizon "insufficiently planetary." And the questions raised *über die Line*—over the line—portend struggles in comparison with which "world wars remain superficial." Perhaps . . . Our reading of Gracq with Jünger has attempted, nevertheless, to redeem Heidegger's text from its residue of metaphysics by affirming the extent to which the displacements of the Line have proliferated historically between and within French and German. To enter into what Heidegger on Jünger crosses out as the B~~ei~~ng of nihilism is to broach the capacity of each of those tongues to pry open the distance that separates the other *from itself*. To observe that proliferation in—or as—the text of history *per se* is, then, one horizon afforded by the *grand jeu* initiated by Julien Gracq.

APPENDIX II

A version of the first chapter of this book, "Blanchot at *Combat*: Literature and Terror," originally appeared in *MLN* (May 1980). In June 1982, a frequently confused and confusing French translation of that essay was published by *Tel quel* (92) and immediately found an advocate (B.-H. Lévy, *Le Matin*, 22 June 1982) and a critic (M. Bénézet, *La Quinzaine littéraire*, 1–15 July 1982) in the French press. My own contribution to the debate occasioned by the *Tel quel* version was a letter to the editor of *La Quinzaine littéraire*, which follows in translation:

Boston, 24 September 1982

Maurice Nadeau, Director
La Quinzaine littéraire
43, rue du Temple
75004 Paris
FRANCE

Sir:

I have only just read the indignant page by Mathieu Bénézet occasioned by the publication in *Tel quel* of a translation of my article "Blanchot at *Combat*: Literature and Terror" (*MLN*, May 1980). I appear therein as an American agent commissioned by the Célinophiles of *Tel quel* for a "rap in the teeth" [*cassage de gueule*] they themselves would never have dared to deliver. Whereby my text — and the enigma of the political writings of Blanchot before the war — are presumably placed in their proper context. It is on that general subject that I would like to offer several clarifications.

APPENDIX II

First, if indeed there has been a *cassage de gueule* in this affair, it is the one inflicted by the translator on my text. I was not able to see the French version until after it had appeared, and immediately transmitted to the editor of the journal—in a letter I asked him to include in a forthcoming issue—my shock at the sheer number of blunders disfiguring the essay. I refer not to any inevitably betrayed nuances, but to actual inversions of my thought. Those errors, I should say, were by no means intentional; a slight ignorance of English, I observed, was sufficient in all cases.

Having said as much, I would like to respond, nevertheless, to several remarks by M. Bénézet. At the heart of his indignation is my use of the word *anti-Semite*: "No one can maintain that he [Blanchot] was an anti-Semite, as is done in this article: *'Blanchot's own liquidation of an anti-Semitic past'*! It's written, so I ask: where is the proof? What quotations?" I shall limit myself to two particularly painful passages:

1. "The shameful Sarraut government, which seems to have received the mission of humiliating France as it had not been humiliated in twenty-five years, has driven this disorder to a pitch. It has said everything that should not have been said; it has done nothing of what should have been done. It began by hearing the appeals of unfettered revolutionaries and Jews, whose theological furor demanded against Hitler all possible sanctions immediately. Nothing could be as dangerous or senseless as that delirium of verbal energy. Nothing could be as perfidious as that propaganda for national honor, executed by foreigners suspected by the offices of the Quai d'Orsay, to precipitate young Frenchmen, in the name of Moscow or Israel, into an immediate conflict . . ." This text, quoted in the article, is drawn from "Après le coup de force germanique" (*Combat* 1, no. 4, April 1936).

2. Concerning "the detestable character of what is called with solemnity the Blum experiment," Blanchot (in *Combat* 1, no. 7, July 1936, "Le terrorisme, méthode de salut publique") writes: "A splendid union, a holy alliance, this conglomerate of Soviet, Jewish, and capitalist interests. All that is antinational, all that is antisocial will be served." And then: "It is good, it is beautiful that these people—who believe they have all power, who make use as they wish of justice and laws, who appear to be the veritable masters of the beautiful blood of France [*du beau sang français*]—suddenly experience their weaknesses and that they be called by fear back to reason."

M. Bénézet, moreover, who is sensitive to the presence of Céline's name in the columns of *Tel quel*, appears not to know that Drumont was one of the four or five authors whose "texts to reread" were heartily recommended by *Combat* (*Combat* 3, no. 21, January 1938).

The depressing reality of the texts—the more violent of which was quoted in my article—has quite simply been expunged. May I suggest that that denial finds a curious echo in the following sentence of M. Bénézet: "And without xenophobia—and if the disavowal seems suspect, so be it!—why go search out an American professor . . ."? For it is as though one were reading a recycled version of a (barely imaginable) sentence by Blanchot writing in an article of 1932 that the "poetry" of French letters was in the last analysis forbidden "to foreigners and to a number of Frenchmen as foreign as they" (*La Revue française*, 27 May 1932, "La Culture française vue par un Allemand"). France for the French, and even in her texts!

Finally, I would like to insist that the aim of my essay was by no means retribution. It simply appeared to me dishonest to praise piously, say, the dimension of the heterogeneous in the writings of one of the great writers of the century, I agree, while deleting the most unassimilable fragment of his oeuvre. All of which, I learn from the *Quinzaine*, will not prevent this kind of distortion from continuing. I am certain, for my part, that the understanding of what Blanchot has recently called "le combat pour ne pas nommer le combat" will hardly be advanced by those who do battle to prevent any mention of *Combat*.

Frenchmen, if you only knew [*Français, si vous saviez*] . . . English, for example . . .

J. M.

La Quinzaine littéraire chose not to publish this response as long as I insisted on retaining the quotations from Blanchot. It was printed in its entirety in the first issue of the journal *L'Infini* (January 1983).

NOTES

NOTES

Introduction

1. The role of Blanchot and Lacan in recent French thought is self-evident, immense, and in need of no comment. The "influence" exercised by Giraudoux and Gide, since their respective deaths, has receded. Yet it is sufficient to observe the role played by Gide in *Roland Barthes* (by Roland Barthes; Paris: Seuil, 1974) or by Giraudoux in Claude Roy, *Moi je: Essai d'autobiographie* (Paris: Gallimard, 1969) to realize at what proximity to contemporary criticism and creation in France their respective *oeuvres*, however apparently in eclipse, continue to function.

2. The entire development can be captured in a series of quotations. First, Charles Vildrac, in his *Pages de journal*, relaying the exclamation of a French society matron during the early stages of World War II: "Here's to a rapid victory, so we can again be anti-Semites!" (quoted in C. Wardi, *Le Juif dans le roman français, 1933–1948*; Paris: Nizet, 1973, p. 62). (Unless otherwise indicated, all translations from the French in this volume are my own.) After the war, however, the discovery of the extent of Hitler's atrocities resulted in a radical suspension of that wish. Thus the law laid down by Sartre in 1954: "Anti-Semitism does not enter into the category of thoughts protected by the right of free speech" (*Réflexions sur la question juive*; Paris: Gallimard, 1954, p. 10). The more prescient of French anti-Semites, however, even before the war, intuited that the damage Hitler was inflicting on their cause was irreversible. Whence the anxiety one senses Bernanos fending off in 1938: "If it pleases M. Hitler to dishonor at present the cause my old Master [Drumont] served, what difference does it make?" ("A propos de l'antisémitisme de Drumont" in *La Grande Peur des bien-pensants*; Paris: Livre de poche, 1969, p. 436.)

3. The recent debate over A. Fabre-Luce's *Pour en finir avec l'antisémitisme* (Paris: Julliard, 1979) shows to what an extent a certain anti-Semitism can thrive parasitically on the motif of "the end of anti-Semitism." Fabre-Luce's argument in large part is that anti-Semitism is horrendous and would long since have disappeared in France were it not for the annoying habit of the Jews to insist that Vichy's attitude toward them was anything less than benign. An admirable corrective to Fabre-Luce's book is M. Marrus and R. Paxton, *Vichy et les Juifs* (Paris: Calmann-Lévy, 1981). (An American edition, *Vichy and the Jews*, was published by Basic Books, New York, in 1982.)

4. The story appears as the epigraph of Patrick Modiano's novel *La Place de l'Etoile* (Paris: Gallimard, 1968). The book is a hallucinatory mock-carnival of prewar French anti-Semitism, featuring among its characters Céline, Brasillach, Drieu, and Rebatet. I suspect that the book's immense success in France had less to do with its intrinsic merits than with the

possibility it offered of plunging innocently into a taboo thematic under the guidance of an author of the most impeccable political credentials: he was born in 1947. That circumstance, curiously, is the obverse of the situation obtaining in the case of George Steiner's macabre, mock-Messianic *tour de force*, *The Portage to San Cristóbal of A. H.* (New York: Simon and Schuster, 1981), a fantasy of international intrigue surrounding the capture and retrieval of a decrepit Hitler, aged ninety, from the Amazonian jungle. For that work exudes a sense of the ultimate (intellectual, moral) frivolity of anyone too *young* to have known — on one side or the other — the horrors of Hitlerism.

5. L. Poliakov, *Histoire de l'antisémitisme* (Paris: Calmann-Lévy, 1977), vol. 4, p. 332. Poliakov quotes from G. Vacher de Lapouge's *"Dies irae* — la fin du monde civilisé," *Europe* (October 1923). "Senile Europe has learned nothing, forgotten nothing. The old days continue. We steal, we slaughter, wholesale and retail. . . . We ham it up . . . pilgrimage . . . devour a few Jesuits . . . keep things the same. . . . Syphilis reigns and the *bistro* governs . . . ." On Vacher de Lapouge's racism, see Z. Sternhell, *La Droite révolutionnaire, 1885-1914: Les Origines françaises du fascisme* (Paris: Seuil, 1978), pp. 158-71.

6. See Sternhell, *La Droite révolutionnaire*, p. 164.

7. See my "On Tear-work: *l'ar de Valéry*" in *Yale French Studies* (1976), as well as my "Craniometry and Criticism: Notes on a Valeryan Criss-cross" in *Boundary 2* (April 1983).

8. Valéry, it may be noted, sent a sum of money, "not without reflection," to Drumont's *La Libre Parole* as part of the campaign in 1898-99 to honor the memory of Commandant Henry, who had recently committed suicide after his role in the fraudulent inculpation of Dreyfus had been discovered. See Sternhell, *La Droite révolutionnaire*, p. 155.

9. It is perhaps useful at this juncture to state that none of the four writers considered has ever been accused to my knowledge of collaborationism during the war, and one, Blanchot, had important ties to the Resistance.

10. Such sensationalism is the most egregious shortcoming of B. H. Lévy's *L'Idéologie française* (Paris: Grasset, 1981). His general project — of articulating R. Paxton's argument (that Vichy was frequently one step ahead of Germany in its politics of repression) with Z. Sternhell's (that French thought provided the intellectual matrix out of which European fascism emerged) — is nevertheless provocative and eminently worthy of being pursued. See R. Paxton, *Vichy France* (New York: Norton, 1972) and Z. Sternhell, *La Droite révolutionnaire*.

11. G. Scholem, *On Jews and Judaism in Crisis* (New York: Schocken, 1976), p. 72.

I. Blanchot at *Combat*: Of Literature and Terror

1. "Vivre autrement le temps," *Le Nouvel Observateur*, 30 April 1979.

2. See the notes of Joseph Jurt to the Pléiade edition of *La Grande Peur* in *Essais et écrits de combat* (Paris: Gallimard, 1971), vol. 1, p. 1369.

3. See Z. Sternhell, *La Droite révolutionnaire, 1885-1914: Les Origines françaises du fascisme* (Paris: Seuil, 1978), chapter 4, "L'Antisémitisme de gauche," pp. 177-214. In *La Libre Parole* of 26 April 1899, Drumont, a *député* representing Algiers, could write: "I regularly voted with the extreme Left, with the socialists, for all those measures that constituted a social reform or would result in an amelioration of the workers' fate. I split with the socialists only on questions of patriotism."

4. For Barrès, in *L'Appel au soldat* (Paris: Fasquelle, 1900, p. 465), anti-Semitism constituted "the people's formula" *par excellence*. Still later, Maurras would write in *Action française*, 28 March 1911: "All would seem impossible, or frightfully difficult, without the providential arrival of anti-Semitism. With it, everything falls smoothly and simply into place. If one were not an anti-Semite out of patriotism, one would become one out of opportunism."

5. For Sorel's theory of myths, see his *Réflexions sur la violence* (Paris: Rivière, 1972), "Introduction," pp. 26-58. For a discussion of Sorel's curious incursions into anti-Semitism, see I. L. Horowitz's *Radicalism and the Revolt of Reason* (Carbondale: Southern Illinois University Press, 1961), pp. 39-41.

6. In *The Marquis de Morès: Emperor of the Bad Lands* (Norman: University of Okalahoma Press, 1970, p. 3), D. Dresden glorifies him as "the most celebrated and the most shot-at man in the history of the Bad Lands of Dakota Territory."

7. Morès, *Le Secret des changes* (Marseille: Imprimerie marseillaise, 1894), p. 84. See as well Sternhell, *La Droite révolutionnaire*, pp. 180-84, 197-220.

8. The imaginative importance for Bernanos of Morès's fate (in his relations with the financier Herz) can be gauged by the impression the author gives of virtually *acting out* Morès's humiliation in his own dealings with François Coty several years later. The episode was at the center of Bernanos's break with the Action française, and figures centrally in the campaign launched by Maurras, L. Daudet, and Pujo against Bernanos, "dandy de la mangeoire." See H. Guillemin, *Regards sur Bernanos* (Paris: Gallimard, 1976), p. 84.

9. See Bernanos, *Les Enfants humiliés* in *Essais et écrits de combat*, vol. 1.

10. Of *La Grande Peur*, J.-L. Loubet del Bayle writes: "The book . . . in fact appeared to the young men grouped around *Réaction* as the most faithful expression of their feelings of revolt toward the middle class France of the Third Republic," in *Les Non-conformistes des années 30: Une Tentative de renouvellement de la pensée politique française* (Paris: Seuil, 1969), p. 68. For Blanchot's contributions to *Réaction*, see the bibliography in *Gramma* 3-4 (1976), p. 225.

11. A facsimile edition of *Les Cahiers du Cercle Proudhon* has been printed by the Centre d'Etudes de l'Agora (Paris, 1976). On the violence of anti-Jewish sentiment in Proudhon's *Carnets*, see L. Poliakov, *Histoire de l'antisémitisme* (Paris: Calmann-Lévy, 1981), vol. 2., pp. 207-11.

12. Bernanos, *Essais et écrits de combat*, vol. 1, pp. 385-86.

13. Quoted in P. Andreu, "Fascisme 1913" in *Combat* 1, no. 2 (February 1936).

14. See Sternhell, *La Droite révolutionnaire*, pp. 392-400. Sternhell's thesis, striking in its timeliness, reads (p. 24): "In fact, of all the new currents of thought, schools and systems, it was Marxism that penetrated least deeply, most slowly in France. . . . If Germany was the homeland of orthodox Marxism, France was the laboratory in which the original syntheses of the twentieth century were forged." Those "syntheses" were the matrix of what would later emerge as fascism.

15. For a discussion of Thierry Maulnier's political evolution, see P. Sérant, *Les Dissidents de l'Action française* (Paris: Copernic, 1978), pp. 299-344.

16. Maulnier's codirector of *Combat* was Jean de Fabrègues, who subsequently authored *Bernanos tel qu'il était* (Paris: Mame, 1963). "Fascisme 1913" by P. Andreu appeared in *Combat* 1, no. 2 (February 1936).

17. Invoking the break in the career of Bertrand de Jouvenel occasioned by the war, P. Andreu writes: "Few men have changed as much — perhaps Maurice Blanchot — intellectually and morally," in *Le Rouge et le blanc, 1928-1944* (Paris: La Table Ronde, 1977), p. 86. See as well Claude Roy, *Moi je* (Paris: Gallimard, 1969), p. 233, for a recollection of Blanchot arriving — "a quite diaphanous and fragile apparition" — at gatherings of *Combat* at La Coupole.

18. *Le Rouge et le blanc*, p. 122.

19. *Combat* 1, no. 9. Writing of Blanchot's literary works, J. Derrida, in "Pas," comments on the disseminative action of Blanchot's "double pas" throughout his titles: *Faux pas, Le Pas au-delà, L'Espace littéraire, La Part du feu, Celui qui ne m'accompagnait pas*. The move from *Grande Peur* to "Grande Passion" constitutes, then, something of a signature. See "Pas," *Gramma* 3-4 (1976), pp. 144-45.

20. *Combat* 1, no. 9. Compare Bernanos, in *La Grande Peur*, on Boulangism: "But our right-wingers [*les gens de droite*] thought they detected the scent of a master, and were already presenting their buttocks. Only instead of the voluptuous beating they expected they were treated to a cold shower." (*Essais et écrits de combat*, vol. 1, p. 188.)

21. See *Les Grands Cimetières sous la lune* in *Essais et écrits de combat*, vol. 1, p. 409.

22. Bernanos, *La Grande Peur*, p. 110.

23. "Après le coup de force germanique" in *Combat* 1, no. 4 (April 1936).

24. "La France, nation à venir" in *Combat* 2, no. 19 (November 1937).

25. Blanchot, "La Fin du 6 février" in *Combat* 1, no. 2 (February 1936): "That great and painful date is now no more than a symbol. It is time, in the order of revolt, to think of something different than pious commemorations."

26. "Après le coup de force germanique." In Blanchot's terms, of course, Georges Mandel did pay; he was murdered by the Collaborationist Milice on 6 July 1944.

27. "Le Terrorisme, méthode de salut publique" in *Combat* 1, no. 7 (July 1936).

28. Published by José Corti.

29. Blanchot, "Comment la littérature est-elle possible?" p. 10.

30. Ibid., p. 24.

31. Ibid., p. 14.

32. Ibid., p. 15.

33. Blanchot, *Faux pas* (Paris: Gallimard, 1943), p. 352.

34. Paulhan, *Les Fleurs de Tarbes ou la Terreur dans les lettres* (Paris: Gallimard, 1941), p. 58, "La Terreur trouve son philosophe."

35. "It is curious to observe to what extent the reflections of Bergson concerning language—and that fragile and perpetually reinstituted language: literature—have *become* true" (*Les Fleurs de Tarbes*, p. 59).

36. See the diverse commentaries in the *Hommage à Georges Sorel* in the third and fourth *Cahiers du Cercle Proudhon* (May-August 1912).

37. See Horowitz, *Radicalism and the Revolt of Reason*, pp. 39–56.

38. "Comment la littérature est-elle possible?" p. 11.

39. Ibid., p. 24.

40. G. Deleuze and M. Foucault, "Les Intellectuels et le pouvoir" in *L'Arc*, no. 49, p. 8.

41. Blanchot, *L'Amitié* (Paris: Gallimard, 1971), p. 179. According to Loubet del Bayle, *Les Non-conformistes*, p. 458, Blanchot's last political endeavor before launching his "second career" was to serve quite briefly as a literary director of Jeune France, "a cultural association sponsored by the Secrétariat général à la jeunesse de Vichy." It is illuminating in this context—fascist terrorism disarticulated by the infernal machine it is predicated against—to recall the reaction to Vichy of Lucien Rebatet in *Les Décombres, 1938-1940* (Paris: Pauvert, 1976), p. 540: "As the whole Parliament began unpacking, there swooped down on Vichy a host of committeemen, electoral agents, unlicensed journalists, blackmailers, the full cohorts of Masonry and the League of the Rights of Man, entire corridors of the Palais-Bourbon, congresses of Radicals and Socialists, general councillors, municipal councillors, 'presidents' by the trainload, suburban Mazarins: the whole regime."

42. *Le Solstice de juin* (Paris: Gallimard, 1976), p. 264.

43. Ibid., p. 263.

44. Ibid., p. 256.

45. We touch here on the diverse and surprising articulations between "French fascism," "collaboration," and "resistance." Concerning Blanchot, Claude Roy—for whom the war served as a conduit from Maurrassian royalism to Stalinism—writes: "During the Resistance, curiously, I would rediscover around or in the Communist party many former Maurrassian 'nationalists,' who could at last breathe freely as both socialists and 'patriots': Claude Morgan, Jean Sabier, Emmanuel d'Astier, Debû-Bridel, Maurice Blanchot. Exceptions, to be sure, but

interesting ones." (In *Moi je* p. 193.) On the other hand, on 18 May 1942, midst "les beaux jours des collabos," in H. Amouroux's phrase, Paul Léautaud telephones Drieu la Rochelle to inquire about rumors of a return to a prewar editorship of the *N.R.F.*, and notes in his journal Drieu's response: "'There's not a word of truth in all that. It's pure gossip, fiction. The only thing that is exact is that I go somewhat less to the journal. I felt a bit tired by all the work I had performed for it. I also have work to do for myself. So I stationed a secretary there, this M. Blanchot. . . . That's the whole truth.' I told him: 'It's that Paulhan himself has said to certain people . . .' – Yes, yes, I know, he was taking his wishes for reality. – I was also astonished that the 'Occupants' would accept . . . –*Parbleu!*" (*Journal littéraire*; Paris: Mercure de France, 1963, vol. 14 p. 236.) As late as 1942, if we are to believe Léautaud, Blanchot was running the *N.R.F.* as Drieu's surrogate. (By 20 August 1942, Léautaud notes, Drieu had resumed his functions.)

Postscriptum: I submitted the text of this essay to Maurice Blanchot in manuscript form. His reaction, in a letter of 26 November 1979, was one of utter disagreement with my argument. From that letter I quote the single "rectification" proposed. It concerns (without mentioning) the quotation from Léautaud in the above note: "I will indicate in only one (admittedly exemplary) case the way in which things may be reversed according to the intentions they are made to signify. You suggested that I was the representative of Drieu at the *nrf*, the collaborator of a notorious [*insigne*] collaborator. But what happened was precisely the opposite. After I resigned from 'Jeune France,' in which I remained only a few weeks (having seen, with a few friends, how naive and dangerous it was to want to use Vichy against Vichy), Jean Paulhan, with whom I was closely associated, asked me to meet with Drieu, whom I knew very slightly. The latter, who was not unaware of which side I was on, offered to me the 'free' directorship of the *nrf*, the journal again becoming purely literary, he himself no longer taking care of it [*ne s'en occupant plus*], but remaining nominally in charge as a safeguard. What was his intention? I sensed that it was dangerous: with the journal again becoming innocent, it would be a matter of attracting writers that the discredited name of Drieu repelled. I asked him to be allowed to delay my answer. I informed Paulhan of the situation. It was essential, he said, to gain time. He perhaps dreamed (without any illusion) of a journal having a certain subversive potential. That seemed to me a trap [*leurre*]. He then consulted a certain number of 'great' writers in order to form an editorial committee for the journal; I mention a few that I recall: Claudel, Valéry, Gide, Schlumberger, Paulhan, Mauriac. I failed to see what assurance they would bring. I saw, rather, how they would be compromised (as poor Alain, so ill and so lacking in lucidity, had already been). I thought, moreover, that Drieu would refuse. Which is what happened: the name of Mauriac (who had not belonged to the old *nrf*) seemed to him a provocation. He renewed to me his previous offer. I refused absolutely, saying to him: I could not ask writers to collaborate on a journal for which I myself would not want to write. We left each other, and I didn't see him again, except once, at the end of '43 or the beginning of '44, when I met him on the Champs-Elysées. He said to me: 'So it was you who was right. They are really too stupid' (I imagine: the occupants or the collaborators). I answered: 'It's not a matter of stupidity but of horror [*ce n'est pas de la bêtise, c'est de l'horreur*].'"

46. Blanchot, *Faux pas*, p. 84.
47. Ibid., p. 84.
48. Ibid., p. 85.
49. Ibid., p. 47.
50. Ibid., p. 51.
51. Ibid., p. 52.
52. D. Hollier, "La Nuit américaine," in *Poétique* 22 (1975), pp. 227–43.
53. See M. Blanchot, "La Culture française vue par un Allemand,"*La Revue française*, 27 March 1932. In Blanchot's critique of Ernst Robert Curtius, the ideal of French clarity is

attributed alternately to "a kind of universal suffrage" and "to foreigners and a number of Frenchmen who are as foreign as they." It is opposed to a "vivid flame" [*flamme éclatante*], which dazzles . . .

54. Still, see the curious case of Giraudoux, writing *La Folle de Chaillot* during the German occupation of Paris as a fantasy of triumph against an alien "race" of speculators invading Paris. When read in conjunction with the openly anti-Semitic *Pleins pouvoirs* (1939), *La Folle* emerges as a complex *tour de force*: the revenge of Athalie. At the end of his career, Racine offered up an aged version of his heroines (Athalie) trapped by the Jews she sought to destroy. At the end of his, Giraudoux, who had written eloquently of Racine's "vieillarde" in *Littérature*, presents an antiquated *jeune fille* and has her this time pull off the mass extermination at which her predecessor had failed. See "A Future for *Andromaque*: Aryan and Jew in Giraudoux's France," pp. 34-63 of this volume.

55. "L'honneur est ce qui nous rassemble" in *Français si vous saviez* (Paris: Gallimard, 1961), p. 325.

56. See Thierry Maulnier, "Notes sur l'antisémitisme" in *Combat* 3, no. 26 (June 1938): "The Jewish problem must be attacked and resolved in its causes . . ." *L'Honneur d'être juif* (Paris: Laffont, 1971).

57. M. Blanchot, *La Folie du jour* (Paris: Fata Morgana, 1973); E. Lévinas, "Exercices sur 'La Folie du jour'" in *Sur Maurice Blanchot* (Paris: Fata Morgana, 1975).

58. Blanchot, *La Folie*, p. 19.

59. Ibid., p. 21.

60. Lévinas, "Exercices sur 'La Folie du jour,'" p. 67; Blanchot, *La Folie*, p. 30.

61. Blanchot, *La Folie*, p. 28.

62. Ibid., p. 33.

63. Ibid., p. 24.

64. Ibid., p. 25.

65. M. Foucault, *Surveiller et punir* (Paris: Gallimard, 1975). On the dissymmetry between seeing and being seen, see A. Borinsky, *Ver/ser visto* (Barcelona: Bosch, 1978).

66. Lévinas, "Exercices sur 'La Folie du jour,'" p. 60.

67. Ibid., p. 59.

68. Ibid., p. 72.

69. For a remarkable analysis of what has been lost in the process, see D. and J. Rancière. "La Légende des philosophes (les intellectuels et la traversée du gauchisme)" in *Les Révoltes logiques*, special issue: *"Les Lauriers de mai"* (Paris, 1978).

70. A. Glucksmann, *Les Maîtres Penseurs* (Paris: Grasset, 1977).

71. M. Foucault, "La Grande Colère des faits," *Le Nouvel Observateur*, 9 May 1977, p. 84.

72. Ibid., pp. 85-86.

73. Bernanos, *La Grande Peur*, p. 345.

74. See note 12 above.

75. Bernanos, *La Grande Peur*, p. 101. *Combat* 3, no. 21 (January 1938) reproduces this excerpt in its selection from Drumont, "Textes à relire."

76. Foucault, "La Grande Colère," p. 86.

77. Lévinas, "Exercices sur 'La Folie du jour,'" p. 67.

78. Ibid., p. 71.

79. Bernanos, *La Grande Peur*, p. 349.

80. Ibid., p. 349.

81. Ibid., p. 350.

82. Ibid., p. 313.

83. Foucault, *Les Maîtres Penseurs*, pp. 218-19.

84. On the "combined theoretical effect Glucksmann-Clavel," see J. Rancière, "La Bergère au Goulag" in *Les Révoltes logiques* 1 (Winter 1975). Concerning Clavel's confused indebtedness

to Bernanos, in his effort to imagine a *gauchiste* God, see the following attempt to place *"Dieu est Dieu, nom de Dieu!"* (Paris: Grasset, 1976) under the aegis of the Bernanos of *La Grande Peur: "La Grande Peur des bien-pensants* is already written. It was executed as a risk and asked only to be extended to the other camp: I've done that here, with means infinitely inferior to those of my master . . ." (p.141). (The "other camp" is presumably the liberal wing of the Church.)

85. Foucault, "La Grande Colère," p. 86.

86. Bernanos, *La Grande Peur*, p. 123.

87. The case of Clavel's *"Dieu est Dieu, nom de Dieu!"* offers a stunning confirmation here. Written under the specific aegis of the Bernanos of *La Grande Peur* (see note 84 above), the book is nevertheless philosemitic, and ends with a reading from the *Book of the Martyrs of Israel* recounting Jewish weakness, under Antiochus Epiphanus, in seeking assimilation to the surrounding Hellenistic culture. Presumably, the parallel is with the Church courting—or rallying to – the perpetrators of the Goulag. Reference is made to that "mechanism [*engrenage*] of cultural collaboration which begins quite gently and inoffensively with a gymnasium . . . and then . . . and then . . . and then . . . a goulag at the end" (p. 151). The logic of the analogy is that the Jews will soon be concentration camp operators themselves. Unless they are saved from assimilation by the Maccabees, associated through a pun with the *maquis*, who would call them back to their heritage. The story has its coherence, but it overlooks the fact that the Maccabees did not save the Jews from perpetrating a policy of enslavement and/or extermination, but from being its victim. Even as Clavel would glorify the Maccabees, he places the Jews in the role of totalitarian tyrants, thus renewing, unwittingly, the myth that Bernanos received from the author of *La France juive*.

88. *Combat* 2, no. 20 (December 1937).

89. Blanchot, "Comment la littérature est-elle possible?" p. 15.

90. Blanchot, *La Folie du jour*, p. 26.

91. Blanchot, *L'Amitié*, p. 172.

92. Ibid., p. 183.

93. Ibid.

II. The Suture of an Allusion: Lacan with Léon Bloy

1. *Les Quatre Concepts fondamentaux de la psychanalyse* (Paris: Seuil, 1973), pp. 172–73.

2. S. Freud-K. Abraham, *Correspondance* (Paris: Gallimard, 1969), p. 42.

3. Page references in the text are to *Le Salut par les juifs* (Paris: Mercure de France, 1949).

4. See M. Robert, *D'Oedipe à Moïse: Freud et la conscience juive* (Paris: Calmann-Lévy, 1974), p. 223.

5. In *Die Traumdeutung*, trans. J. Strachey (New York: Avon, 1965), p. 229, Freud quotes Jean-Paul: "Which of the two, it may be debated, walked up and down his study with greater impatience after he had formed the plan of going to Rome—Winckelmann, the Vice-Principal, or Hannibal, the Commander in Chief?" On the Freud-Winckelmann nexus, see C. E. Schorske, *Fin-de-siècle Vienna: Politics and Culture* (New York: Knopf, 1980), p. 192.

6. For differing analyses of Freud's relation to Judaism see M. Robert, *D'Oedipe à Moïse*, and D. Bakan, *Sigmund Freud and the Jewish Mystical Tradition* (New York: Schocken, 1965).

7. For a sample of opinion on Bloy in a close associate of Lacan's (during the 1930s), see P. Drieu la Rochelle, *Sur les écrivains*, ed. F. Grover (Paris: Gallimard, 1964), p. 240: "Without Bloy, neither Claudel, nor Bernanos, nor Céline are imaginable. Without Léon Bloy, not a single militant and aggressive virtue of the spirit is imaginable in the literature of the past fifty years. . . . There is in this oeuvre, with its truncated powers, something of an amputee's stump [*moignon*] bearing witness to the unheard of resources of man. . . . This miserable man of letters, racked by pride, humiliated by vanity, to the extent that his enormous virtues

are entirely caricatured by his sorry shortcomings, was a soldier, a pauper, a doctor, a prophet, a saint. At last a saint in France after all this time." For Lacan's relations with Drieu, see D. Desanti, *Drieu la Rochelle ou le séducteur mystifié* (Paris: Flammarion, 1978), p. 272. An additional link in the Lacan-Bloy connection is perhaps offered by Borges, "in his oeuvre so harmonious with the *phylum* of our undertaking," as Lacan puts it in his *Séminaire sur "La Lettre volée*," p. 23 of his *Ecrits* (Paris: Seuil, 1966). For Borges's evocation of the metaphor of specularity in Bloy and the vicissitudes of Saint Paul's verse *Videmus nunc per speculum in aenigmate* in his work, see "El espejo de los enigmas" in *Otras inquisiciones* (Buenos Aires: Emecé, 1960). On the Drieu-Borges connection, see Desanti, *Drieu la Rochelle*, pp. 275–78, as well as my introduction to *Les Années 30*, special issues of *MLN* (French, 1980).

8. Drumont's *La France juive* (Paris: Flammarion, 1885) was one of the most profitable publishing endeavors of the century. See Z. Sternhell, *La Droite révolutionnaire, 1885–1914: Les Origines françaises du fascisme* (Paris: Seuil, 1978), pp. 175–85.

9. Bernanos, "Dans l'amitié de Léon Bloy" in *Le Lendemain c'est vous* (Paris: Plon, 1969), p. 239.

10. On the importance of Lacan's prose style to his project, see "La Psychanalyse et son enseignement" in *Ecrits*, p. 458: "Any return to Freud resulting in a teaching worthy of the name will occur only on the path through which the most hidden truth becomes manifest in the revolutions of culture. That path is the only formation that we might pretend to transmit to those who follow us. It is called: a style."

11. For a discussion of the history of psychoanalysis in these terms, see my introduction to *French Freud* (*Yale French Studies* 48).

12. An entry in the table of contents of Lacan's *Ecrits*, in the section "L'Idéologie de la libre-entreprise," reads: "American Way of Life." Lacan's critique of America is generally assumed to come from the "left" of liberalism. Yet it is far from clear that Lacan's anti-Americanism does not share roots with that of Bloy's disciple, Georges Bernanos. See, for example, the end of *La Grande Peur des bien-pensants*, quoted above, p. 19.

13. For a discussion of the resistance to figural interpretation and anti-Jewish polemics, see E. Auerbach, "Figura" in *Scenes from the Drama of European Literature* (New York: Meridian, 1959), p. 40: "Thus Augustine: 'For the Lord spoke not idly . . . when He told the Jews, saying: "Had ye believed Moses, you would have believed Me, for he wrote of Me." For those men accepted the Law in a carnal sense, and did not understand its earthly promises as types (*figuras*) of heavenly things' (*De civitate*, 20, 28)."

14. Ultimately, the force — and piquancy — of Bloy's position lies in combining the two temporalities: the dissolution of history in the fulfillment of figures, and the delays in the revelation of that dissolution, what Albert Béguin calls "the paradox of impatient patience" (in *Léon Bloy, mystique de la douleur*; Paris: Labergerie, 1948, p. 82). Elsewhere, Béguin finds himself analyzing the (same) paradox implicit in the following sentence: "It is only time that is needed [*ce n'est que du temps qu'il faut*] for the solvent Master of Eternity, and time is made of the desolation of men" (p. 38). For a discussion of a similar temporal duplicity in Lacan, mediated by the phrase *faut-le-temps*, see my "The Floating Signifier: From Lévi-Strauss to Lacan" in *French Freud*.

15. On the general subject of psychoanalysis and figural interpretation, in lieu of an articulation, consider the perspective offered by two sentences: 1) "The strangely new meaning [phenomenal prophecy] of *figura* in the Christian world is first to be found in Tertullian, who uses it frequently." (From Auerbach, "Figura.") 2) "We have had sexuality since the eighteenth century and sex since the nineteenth. What we had before that was no doubt the flesh. The basic originator of it all was Tertullian." (From Michel Foucault, "The Confession of the Flesh" in *Power/Knowledge*, ed. C. Gordon; New York: Pantheon, 1980, p. 211.)

16. Pp. 42-43: "to love them *as such* [*comme tels*] is a proposition revolting to nature."

17. Sartre, *Réflexions sur la question juive* (Paris: Gallimard, 1954).

18. Ibid., p. 71.

19. Ibid., p. 67.

20. Lacan, *Les Quatre Concepts fondamentaux de la psychanalyse*, p. 163.

21. See my "Poe *pourri*: Lacan's Purloined Letter" in *Semiotexte* 3 (1975), reprinted in *Aesthetics Today*, ed. P. Gudel (New York: New American Library, 1980). The three instances in Lacan's analysis of Poe's tale are: 1) a deluded objectivity (the king, the police, ego psychology); 2) a deluded subjectivity (the queen, then the minister, narcissism; 3) the "objectality" of the unconscious (Dupin, the analyst).

22. Paris: P.U.F., 1952. It is perhaps worth noting that Loewenstein refers to Bloy only once, in passing, p. 131, on the interdependence of Christian and Jew.

23. Lacan, *Les Quatre Concepts fondamentaux de la psychanalyse*, p. 39.

24. *Moses and Monotheism* (New York: Vintage, 1955), p. 117. "We must not forget that all the peoples who now excel in the practice of anti-Semitism became Christians only in relatively recent times, sometimes forced to it by bloody compulsion. One might say they are all 'badly christened'; under the thin veneer of Christianity they have remained what their ancestors were, barbarically polytheistic. They have not yet overcome their grudge against the new religion which was forced on them, and have projected it on to the source from which Christianity came to them."

25. See Bakan, *Sigmund Freud and the Jewish Mystical Tradition*, p. 156, in which the Jew is seen as symbolic of the superego. Bakan, ultimately less convincing but more suggestive than Robert, sees Freud as a crypto-Kabbalist, fulfilling the "Sabbatian, i.e., mystical-messianic mood in modern dress" (p. 153). Concerning Freud's anonymous analysis of Michelangelo's statue, the brunt of the interpretation is to disarm the prophet's wrath: "the Moses we have constructed," writes Freud in his text of 1914, "will neither leap up nor cast the Tables from him." (Freud, "The Moses of Michelangelo" in his *On Creativity and the Unconscious*; New York: Harper and Row, 1958, p.33.)

26. *Speculation*, it may be noted, is the term in Freud around which Derrida has assembled his recent investigations into psychoanalysis. See "Spéculer—sur Freud" in *La Carte postale: de Socrate à Freud et au-delà* (Paris: Aubier-Flammarion, 1980), p. 283: "Speculation: what is thus designated by Freud focuses the entire difficulty which interests me at this juncture. What does philosophy *not have to do* [literally: to see, *à voir*] with psychoanalytic 'speculation'?

27. The temporality of *Nachträglichkeit* (*après-coup*) is, of course, part and parcel of figural interpretation. Thus the Abraham-Iscariot repetition is prepared by: "But the 'worm' [*ver*] of their damnation was already gnawing at them *from within* for a very long time before it appeared" (p. 161).

28. M. Riffaterre, "La Trace de l'intertexte" in *La Pensée* 215 (October 1980), p. 9: "The relation of a sign to its object is not direct: it is effected through the mediation of an idea of the object, prompted by the sign, and which itself takes the form of another sign, the interpretant, a partial equivalent of the first. Let us apply this model to intertextuality: the sign of the semiotic relation will in this case be the text, the object will be the intertext, and the interpretant will be a presupposition preventing the text from being nothing but the undifferentiated repetition of its intertext."

29. See "Family Romances" (1908), originally included in Otto Rank's *Mythus von der Geburt des Helden* (Vienna: F. Deuticke, 1909).

30. The incongruity between Freud and Bloy is patent in the case of the allusion to *Le Salut par les juifs*. On the other hand, a consideration of the project of the protagonist of Bloy's autobiographical novel, *Le Désespéré* — the revelation of the illusions of the ego through

the dazzling exegesis of the world considered as a vertiginous text — reveals a basis for an attempt to articulate the break each made with the academic psychology of the *fin de siècle*. Caïn Marchenoir, Bloy's *alter ego*, would found a new science (of history) "which genius alone would be able to save from being ridiculous" (Paris: Mercure de France, 1964, p. 131). History would be revealed as "a homogeneous text — extremely connected [*lié*], articulated [*vertébré*], skeletalized [*ossaturé*], dialecticized [*dialectiqué*], but completely concealed, and that it would be necessary to transcribe into a potentially accessible grammar" (p. 132). The historian, like Freud's analyst, is a cryptographer, and the road of history, like the text of a dream, is composed "entirely of intersections with weathervanes for signposts . . ." (p. 135). The principal casualty of his research is the specular ego: "Fragmentary history . . . is a mirror for the stupid pride of that freedom which endlessly congratulates itself on having done what it intended . . . and the absolute synthesis which I plan confiscates straightway that cosmetic prop in order to force the old hedonist [la *vieille jouisseuse*] to contemplate herself in the very humble sewer-stream that is her homeland" (p. 133).

As for the Lacan-Bloy connection, I suspect it comes closest to explicit formulation in the passage in *Télévision* where Lacan assimilates psychoanalyst and saint: "Let's come then to the psychoanalyst. . . . For we could not situate him any better, objectively, than in terms of what, in the past, was called: being a saint. A saint, during his life, does not impose the respect that occasionally earns him a halo. . . . A saint, let me be understood, does not perform charity [*ne fait pas la charité*]. Rather, he takes to playing the derelict, the outcast [*plutôt se met-il à faire le déchet*]: *il décharite* . . . It is through the abjection of that cause, in fact, that the subject in question has a chance at least to locate its bearings [*se repérer*] in a structure . . ." (p. 28). The pun neologism *décharite* seems to pick up Bloy's notorious attack on the going notion of charity in his article of exultation on the fire of May 1897 that destroyed the Bazar de la Charité. As for the attribution of structural causation to the abject, the willingness to identify with it, such, after all, is the horizon of *Le Salut par les juifs*. It should not be forgotten that Cain, in his murderousness, is a figure of the Jew in that work, and that the name attributed to Bloy's *alter ego*, *le désespéré*, as we have seen, is Caïn Marchenoir. (For Drieu la Rochelle's evocation of Bloy as a saint, see note 7 above.)

31. *The Letters of Sigmund Freud*, ed. Ernst Freud, trans. T. and J. Stern (New York: MacGraw-Hill, 1964), p. 17.

32. See Derrida, "Spéculer — sur Freud."

33. "Beyond the pleasure principle," beyond a certain relation to Judaism, but beyond the principle of identity (or principle?) itself. The merchant's imperative of (Jewish) pleasure reads: "The Jew is made for joy [*Freude*] and joy [*Freude*] for the Jew."

34. See *Moses and Monotheism*, part 3, section 2, chapter 4, "The Truth in Religion."

35.   Nathan, heisst du Jude?
                                (Ein seltsamer Jude am)
                                Sprich weiter, wackerer Nathan.

Freud, quoting from memory, approximates Nathan's encounter with Saladin in act 3, scene 5.

36. *Moses and Monotheism*, p. 140. "Without doubt it must have been a tremendous father image that stooped in the person of Moses to tell the poor Jewish laborers that they were his dear children."

37. See *The Interpretation of Dreams*, p. 230. Freud on his father: "Thus it was, on one such occasion, that he told me a story to show how much better things were now than they had been in his days. 'When I was a young man,' he said, 'I went for a walk on Saturday in the streets of your birthplace; I was well dressed and had a new fur cap on my head. A Christian came up to me and with a single blow knocked off my cap into the mud and shouted: "Jew! get off the pavement!"' 'And what did you do?' I asked. 'I went into the roadway and picked up my cap,' was his quiet reply." Freud's dissatisfaction with his father's reaction

leads him to contrast his own father with Hannibal's (Hamilcar Barca), who made his son swear vengeance on the Romans.

38. In "Family Romance," p. 45, Freud insists that "the new and aristocratic parents are equipped with attributes that are derived entirely from real recollections of the actual and humble ones." Thus, in our reading, the repetition of the gesture of "stooping."

39. Freud is close to admitting the compulsive, unconscious component in *Moses and Monotheism* in part 3, section 2, p. 133. "A work grows as it will and sometime confronts its author as an independent, even an alien creation." In this context, one is inclined to seek an articulation of Freud's discussion of "the postponement and the beginning twice over of sexual life" (p. 94) in the book and his comments on "the unusual way in which this book came to be written: In truth it has been written twice over" (p. 131).

40. In "L'Instance de la lettre dans l'inconscient," *Ecrits*, p. 509, Lacan recommends Leo Strauss's *Persecution and the Art of Writing* (Glencoe: Free Press, 1952), a meditation on the "connaturalité" — in the case of Maimonides, Jehuda ha-Levi, and Spinoza — between that art and that condition. Paradoxically, by the time the *Ecrits* were published, it was the tradition of Bloy — rather than that of Jewish esoterism — that no longer dare reveal itself.

41. *Ecrits*, p. 41.

Postscriptum: This essay is the second of two on the prehistory of the discourses of French (post)modernity. The first — "Blanchot at *Combat*: Of Literature and Terror," pp. 6–22 of this book — dealt with Maurice Blanchot's political writings of the 1930s. For this reason we would conclude these pages by evoking the snide joviality of a short article in a 1938 issue of the journal *Aux écoutes*. Entitled "Freud à Paris," the article deals with Freud's passage through Paris on his way to exile and death in London, providing a record of his own final experience of "French Freud." Somewhere between Freud and Lacan, then; between the first and second writings of *Moses and Monotheism*, we read: "It is not the first time that Princesse Georges de Grèce, *née* Marie Bonaparte, has received under her roof Doctor Sigmund Freud. In days gone by, the scientist passed an entire sun-drenched month on his disciple's property at Saint-Tropez. On the beach of Salins, he instructed her in psychoanalysis." The text is anonymous. A few pages away, in a signed necrological note, the journal's *rédacteur en chef*, otherwise unacknowledged, is — exceptionally — identified: Maurice Blanchot.

III. A Future for *Andromaque*: Aryan and Jew in Giraudoux's France

1. Page references in the text to *Littérature* are to the Gallimard Idées re-edition of *Littérature* (Paris: Grasset, 1941).

2. Aragon's "revelation" is reported in *Ce soir*, 20 February 1944.

3. *Je suis partout*, 11 February 1944.

4. See A. Raymond, *Giraudoux devant la victoire et la défaite* (Paris: Nizet, 1963), pp. 141–42.

5. Giraudoux, who twice visited Harvard, was among the first of a line of prestigious French visitors to American universities. The relation seems to have been profound: In 1939, when named *Commissaire général à l'Information*, he surprised many by calling André Morize, Professor of French Literature at Harvard, to be *chef de service*. See J. Body, *Giraudoux et l'Allemagne* (Paris: Didier, 1975), p. 416.

6. C. Mauron, *Le Théâtre de Giraudoux* (Paris: Corti, 1971), p. 146.

7. C. Mauron, *L'Inconscient dans l'oeuvre et la vie de Racine* (Aix: Ophrys, 1957).

8. Mauron, *Giraudoux*, p. 262.

9. Page references in the text to *Judith* are to Giraudoux's *Théâtre*, vol. 1 (Paris: Grasset, 1958).

10. See J. Robichez, *Le Théâtre de Giraudoux* (Paris: S.E.D.S., 1976), pp. 23–24.

11. A. Gide, *Journal*, pp. 1092–93, quoted in Robichez, *Le Théâtre de Giraudoux*, p. 23.

12. H. Bernstein, *Judith* (Paris: *La Petite Illustration*, 9 December 1922).

13. Ibid., Introduction, p. 3.

14. Ibid.

15. Ibid.

16. Ibid.

17. Ibid.

18. L. Rebatet, *Les Tribus du cinéma et du théâtre* (Paris: Nouvelles Editions Françaises, 1941), p. 112.

19. Ibid., p. 111.

20. Interview with Thomas-Meurice in *Je suis partout*, 29 April 1938.

21. One of the surprises to be found in P. M. Dioudonnat, *Je suis partout, 1930–1944: Les Maurrassiens devant la tentation fasciste* (Paris: La Table Ronde, 1973) is the revelation (p. 226) that Giraudoux was (with Montherlant) the most frequently interviewed author in the history of the journal. My own effort in these pages to disengage an implicit politics of Giraudoux's theater was anticipated, to some degree, by Claude Roy in "Politique tirée des écritures profanes," *Je suis partout*, 2 September 1938.

22. In "De siècle à siècle," *Littérature*, p. 163, Giraudoux sees the French romanticism of the 1820s as a titillating farce in which the newly ensconced members of the bourgeoisie dared their sons to "frighten them — in broad daylight(!)"

23. In the novel, Geneviève had been the former wife of Zelten.

24. Page references in the text to *Siegfried* are to *Théâtre*, vol. 1.

25. Page references in the text to the novel are to *Siegfried et le Limousin* (Paris: Grasset, 1922).

26. "Divertissement de Siegfried," *N.R.F.* (July 1928), p. 13.

27. Ibid., p. 14.

28. See Body, *Giraudoux et l'Allemagne*, p. 227.

29. P. Morand, *Giraudoux, Souvenirs de notre jeunesse* (Geneva: La Palatine, 1946), p. 138.

30. Quoted in Body, *Giraudoux et l'Allemagne*, p. 230.

31. Body, *Giraudoux et l'Allemagne*, p. 230.

32. "Bellac et la tragédie," *Littérature*, p. 233.

33. G. Valois, "Sorel et l'architecture social," *Cahiers du Cercle Proudhon* (May-August 1912), p. 111. See Z. Sternhell, *La Droite révolutionnaire, 1885–1914: Les Origines françaises du fascisme* (Paris: Seuil, 1978), pp. 348–400.

34. See Body, *Giraudoux et l'Allemagne*, p. 223. Du Fresnois was the drama critic of *La Revue critique des idées et des livres*, whose mix of Maurras and Bergson was finely attuned to the Maurras-Sorel link of the Cercle Proudhon. In this light, it is worth observing that Henry Bernstein was a frequent target of the journal. Pierre Gilbert's long piece, "Le Juif dans le théâtre de M. Bernstein: Essai de critique psychologique," 1912, was published under the auspices of du Fresnois.

35. See my "Blanchot at *Combat*: Of Literature and Terror," pp. 6–9 of this book.

36. Quoted in P. Andreu, "Fascisme 1913," *Combat* 1, no. 2 (February 1936).

37. *La Révolution nationale*, 19 February 1944. Alain Laubreaux, in a review of *Ondine*, *Je suis partout*, 7 July 1939: "From M. Giraudoux to Robert Brasillach, the path has been traced. We welcome with special delight that certainty." Laubreaux, who was in all probability the scoundrel he is travestied as in Truffaut's *Le dernier métro*, nevertheless comes closer to the truth of matters than the Sorbonne's Robichez, *Le Théâtre de Giraudoux*, p. 259, who comments that on the subject of Germany, Giraudoux "did not assume as his own the sentence that would prove fatal to Robert Brasillach; he attributed it only to Zelten."

38. *Pleins pouvoirs* (Paris: Gallimard, 1939), p. 84.

39. Ibid., p. 82.

40. Ibid., p. 83.

41. Ibid., p. 82.

42. Bernanos, *Les Grands Cimetières sous la lune* in *Essais et écrits de combat* (Paris: Gallimard, 1971), vol. 1, p. 385.

43. Giraudoux, *Pleins pouvoirs*, p. 121.

44. Ibid., p. 52.

45. Ibid., p. 46.

46. Ibid., p. 59.

47. Ibid., p. 66.

48. Ibid., p. 24.

49. Ibid., p. 76.

50. The scene is printed in *Théâtre*, vol. 1, p. 110.

51. See S. R. Driver, *An Introduction to the Literature of the Old Testament* (New York: Meridian, 1956), p. 437.

52. Page references in the text to *Cantique des cantiques* are to *Théâtre*, vol. 3 (1959).

53. *Eglantine* (Paris: Grasset, 1927), p. 65.

54. Ibid., p. 70.

55. Ibid., p. 60.

56. In *La Guerre de Troie n'aura pas lieu*, *Théâtre*, vol. 2 (1959), p. 264, Hector informs the bellicist Demokos that rubies-for-blood is an unacceptable metaphor. That rejection is discussed by T. J. Kline in the context of "The Crisis of Language in Giraudoux's Theatre," *Romanic Review* 67, no. 2 (March 1976).

57. Giraudoux, *Eglantine*, p. 162.

58. Ibid., p. 163.

59. Ibid., p. 164.

60. Ibid., p. 228.

61. Giraudoux may be situated provocatively in terms of the general historical transition —from a "symbolic of blood" to an "analytic of sexuality"—discussed by M. Foucault on p. 195 of his *Histoire de la sexualité*, vol. I: *La Volonté de savoir* (Paris: Gallimard, 1976). It is tempting to speculate in this context that the polemic of Blood with Sexuality, emerging, for Foucault, at the end of the eighteenth century, recycles *on the left* the conflict of Blood with Money, born—for the Right—with the French Revolution. Giraudoux's incarnation of Blood, Fontranges, is victorious against Money, vanquished by Sexuality.

62. *Bella* (Paris: Grasset, 1926), p. 228.

63. Page references in the text to *Sodome et Gomorrhe* are to *Théâtre*, vol. 4 (1959).

64. Mauron, *Giraudoux*, p. 212.

65. *La Reine de Césarée* (Paris: Plon, 1954), p. 112. "Bérénice: You pursue my past, my name, my family, my age, my nation. Were I not a Jewess, would you bring such zeal to my pursuit?"

66. Act 1, scene 4: He appeared before you in all the radiance of a man/Who bears in his hands the vengeance of Rome./ Judea grew pale . . .

67. Act 1, scene 5: The torches, the stake, the night aflame,/The eagles, the *fasces*, the people, the army . . .

68. Act 2, scene 2: Rome, by a law that cannot be changed,/Admits no foreign blood to mix with its own.

69. Act 5, scene 5: An insulting people/ That makes every recess resound with my misfortune/ Do you not hear it, that cruel joy,/ While I drown, alone, in my tears?/What crime, what offense can motivate them?

70. Act 3, scene 3: Titus loves me. Titus cannot wish my death.

71. See "Quand Vichy déportait ses Juifs: Entretien avec Robert Paxton et Michael Marrus," *Le Nouvel Observateur*, 1–7 June 1981, p. 63.

72. Quoted in Mauron, *Racine*, p. 85.

73. Ibid., p. 86.

74. Marrus and Paxton, *Vichy et les Juifs* (Paris: Calmann-Lévy, 1981). An English-language edition of this work, *Vichy and the Jews*, was published by Basic Books, New York, in 1982.

75. *Le Monde*, 18 February 1977.

76. "Quand Vichy déportait ses Juifs," p. 63.

77. Mauron, *Racine*, p. 85.

78. Compare as well Titus's plaint: "Que sais-je? J'espérais de mourir à vos yeux/Avant que d'en venir à ces cruels adieux" (act 4, scene 5), his hope to die sooner than such sad farewells, with Lia's accusation on p. 73: "In your male hypocrisy and your horror of battles, you would have preferred that death strike us before the truth."

79. In *Vocabulaire de la psychanalyse* (Paris: P.U.F., 1967), p. 383, J. Laplanche and J. B. Pontalis discuss Freud's efforts to identify "ego instincts" [*Ichtriebe*] and "death instincts" [*Todestriebe*].

80. *N.R.F.* (August 1941), quoted in Marrus and Paxton, *Vichy et les Juifs*, p. 65.

81. L. Jouvet in *Opéra*, 12 December 1945: "we will rehearse the play at present and . . . perform it tomorrow, according to the definitive proofs, established after four successive copies, revised and corrected by the author."

82. Page references in the text to *La Folle de Chaillot* are to *Théâtre*, vol. 4.

83. Raymond, *Giraudoux*, p. 139.

84. Alas! if to avenge the shame of Israel,/Our hands cannot, as did formerly Jahel,/Pierce the impious head of the enemies of God,/We can at least sacrifice our life to him.

85. See Mauron, *Racine*, p. 294.

86. Act 3, scene 3: I alone, giving an example to the timid Hebrews,/Deserter of their law, I approved the undertaking,/ And won in the process the priesthood of Baal . . .

87. Act 2, scene 2: In the square before the Temple, reserved for men alone,/ That proud woman enters, her brow raised, /And was even prepared to transgress the limits /Of the sacred precinct . . . (. . .) My Father . . . What fury animated his gaze! (. . .) "Queen, leave," he said, "this formidable site . . ." The queen, then casting a savage eye on him,/No doubt was already opening her mouth in blasphemy . . .

88. Act 2, scene 5: Recovering from my fatal disturbance,/ As I admired his gentleness, his noble and modest manner,/ I suddenly felt a murderous blade/ Whose full length the traitor plunged into my breast.

89. Act 2, scene 7: What new miracle troubles and inhibits me?/The sweetness of his voice, his childlike grace,/Are turning my enmity/To . . . Would I then be sensitive to pity?

90. Act 2, scene 7: I want to share with you all my riches (. . .) I intend to treat you as my son.

91. Act 5, scene 3: . . . as soon as the queen, drunk with mad pride,/ Will have passed the threshold of the Temple,/ She will no longer be able to turn back.

92. As the play ends, we learn more of Adolphe Bertaut, who leads an Edenic cortege of his repentant brethren: "We have decided to vanquish that timidity which has spoiled your life and our own . . ." (p. 178). Of the characters we have already encountered, one thinks of Fontranges, in his impotence, falling asleep, but also, for that reason, of Holophernes, Zelten, and their curtailed solutions to the "Jewish problem." Earlier, in a hallucination, Aurélie confesses to a single act of infidelity: sending one of their cards to General Boulanger.

For Barrès, in *L'Appel au soldat* (Paris: Fasquelle, 1900), p. 466, Boulanger's downfall was his failure to declare himself more forcefully in support of anti-Semitism.

93. See "Nécessité d'une dictature de l'urbanisme," *N.R.F.* (May 1955). Giraudoux's call for a "dictatorship of urbanism" — "Never have the circumstances been more auspicious" — was forwarded to Pétain during the first months of the regime. On the other hand, in *Sans pouvoirs* (Monaco: Editions du rocher, 1946), p. 32, Giraudoux wrote mordantly: "In the leadership institutes [*écoles de chefs*] strewn over the territory, men of gentle character and inoffensive habits assigned themselves the impossible task of depicting as a revolution or earthquake this patriarchal interlude, unaware of the axiom that if the habit of a strong regime may be inculcated in a people, it cannot be taught to its leaders. As early as the first months, it was simple to foresee that the first real power to which the country would be delivered, in the absence of any mobility or revolutionary awareness, would be the one to which it in fact ultimately was: the police." In the context of our reading of *La Folle*, the most striking page in *Sans pouvoirs* (p. 25) is that evoking the Exodus of June 1940: "one of the most beautiful movements that Europe has ever known . . . an outburst of religion to which the Biblical name was immediately affixed." With every Frenchman plunging into dimensions "more French than himself," the "Exodus" — to which Promised Land? — was from the bondage of the Third Republic. Needless to say, from the point of view of the Jews, Giraudoux quite simply inverts the original valence of the Biblical image.

94. M. Blanchot, *Faux pas* (Paris: Gallimard, 1943), p. 113.

95. J.-P. Sartre, *Situations* (Paris: Gallimard, 1947), vol. 1, p. 77.

IV. "Jewish Literature" and the Art of André Gide

1. Gide, "Les Juifs, Céline et Maritain," *N.R.F.* (April 1938), pp. 631-34.

2. L. Daudet, *Action française*, 10 February 1928: "We have, in *Bagatelles pour un massacre*, a polemical tract against the Jews, their power and their maleficence, written with a Rabelaisian vigor, in a language that seems to me superb, chock full of slang, spiced with irony, licentious to say the least, tart, succulent, scatological here, baroque there, always on the mark, always facetious, unequaled in its brilliance. Next to this febrile and unbridled book, Drumont's *La France juive* is a glass of orange-flower water and *Les Juifs rois de l'époque*, by Toussenel, a tale by Berquin. I'll go further still: there does not exist in our literature — since the *Ménipée* and the poems of Agrippa d'Aubigné — a comparable howl of anger, reverberated through the echos of a spoken syntax as muscular, ribald, and bare as a nude by the great Courbet . . ."

3. Gide, "Les Juifs, Céline et Maritain," p. 631.

4. Ibid., pp. 634-35.

5. *Journal, 1889-1939* (Paris: Gallimard, 1951), p. 397.

6. See J. Lacoutoure, *Léon Blum* (Paris: Seuil, 1977), p. 49. The page is quoted as well at the end of L. Rebatet's scurrilous *Les Tribus du théâtre et du cinéma* (Paris: Nouvelles Editions françaises, 1941). On the link between Blum in 1936 and Céline's anti-Semitic writings, see P. Modiano and E. Berl, *Interrogatoire* (Paris: Gallimard, 1976). Berl (p. 82): "When Déat wrote his article 'Mourir pour Dantzig?,' he had half of France with him. People wondered why they should get shot at for Czechs and Poles who couldn't care less for them. So they said it was because of the Jews, and that gave the hysteria of Céline in *Bagatelles pour un massacre*."

7. After World War II, when Blum's sufferings drew the two survivors of their generation closer, Gide would nevertheless write in his *Journal* (9 January 1948): "I am grateful to him for not holding against me the rather harsh passages of my *Journal* on the subject of the Jews and himself (which, moreover, I cannot renounce since I continue to believe them perfectly correct) . . ." *Journal, 1939-1949* (Paris: Gallimard, 1954), p. 320.

8. The *N.R.F.*'s enthusiastic review of *Bagatelles pour un massacre*, by Marcel Arland, a close associate of Gide's, is worth quoting in this context: "And the word *juif* takes on something of the meaning that the word *bourgeois* had in former times. It is in the name of independence, frankness, and lyric emotion that Céline speaks. He does so without nuance, even without equity: confused, scatterbrained [*brouillon*], even false in half of his points . . . Céline's essential position is solid and his voice carries far." It is as though the *N.R.F.* were willing to accept any nonsense as an excuse to sustain Céline's "position." Literary historians tend to speak of a decisive break between Céline's two great novels, on the one hand, and the diatribes that followed. Arland, curiously, proposes a different perspective: "Beyond *Mort à crédit*, whose disenchanted, mechanical, monotonous flow rather quickly became tiresome, the Céline of *Bagatelles* rejoins and prolongs the efforts of the author of the *Voyage*" (*N.R.F.*, February 1938, p. 310).

9. Gide, "Les Juifs, Céline et Maritain," p. 634.

10. In "La querelle du peuplier (*Réponse à M. Maurras*)," *Prétextes* (Paris: Mercure de France, 1947), Gide's dossier on *Les déracinés* turned into a debate on horticultural metaphor: *déracinement, transplantation, repiquage* (the thinning out of seedlings). On the general question of "plants" in Gide, see D. Moutote, *Les Images végétales dans l'oeuvre d' André Gide* (Montpellier: P.U.F., 1970).

11. Page references in the text are to *Les Caves du Vatican* (Paris: Gallimard, 1922).

12. Gide, *Journal, 1889–1939*, p. 440.

13. *Lettres à André Gide* (Neufchatel and Paris: Ides and Calendes, 1949), pp. 24–26.

14. The details of Gide's objections are discussed in G. Painter, *Marcel Proust: A Biography* (London: Chatto and Windus, 1965), vol. 2, p. 188.

15. See my *A Structural Study of Autobiography: Proust, Leiris, Sartre, Lévi-Strauss* (Ithaca: Cornell University Press, 1974), chapter 1.

16. Proust, *A la recherche du temps perdu* (Paris: Gallimard, 1954), vol. 1, p. 37.

17. See in particular the discussion of Proust's assimilation of Odette—*via* Botticelli—to Jethro's daughter in Mehlman, *A Structural Study of Autobiography*, chapter 1.

18. Our reading of the *sotie* functions here in ironic counterpoint to Lacan's delineation of Gide's "aristocratic" vision: "The privilege of a desire besieging the subject can lapse into disuse only once that turn of the labyrinth in which the fire of an encounter has imprinted its blazon is taken up a hundred times again . . . No doubt the seal of that encounter is not only an imprint but a hieroglyph, and from one text can be transferred to others. But no metaphor will ever exhaust its meaning, which is not to have any, to be the mark of that brand which death imparts to flesh once speech [*le verbe*] has extricated it [*death*] from love." ("Jeunesse de Gide," *Ecrits*; Paris: Seuil, 1966, p. 756.)

19. Gide, *Journal des Faux-monnayeurs* (Paris: Gallimard, 1927), p. 18.

20. Ibid., p. 71.

21. The book's principal detractors in 1914 were the Catholic poets Claudel and Jammes. The former wrote to J. Rivière (20 April 1914): "The book is truly sinister, it is as though every sentiment were sullied by it . . ." (Claudel-Gide, *Correspondance, 1889–1926*; Paris: Gallimard, 1949, p. 233). And Jammes to Gide (24 March 1914): "In your last book, not only did you mock my mother the Church in a manner Voltaire would not have risked, and barely even Rémy de Gourmont, but you brought yourself into disrepute . . ." (Ibid., p. 227). In retrospect, the observations on the subject by Julien Gracq (*En lisant en écrivant*; Paris: Corti, 1981, p. 193) seem wryly apposite: "The brandishing of every Catholic shield against Gide shows how much the Catholicism of the beginning of the century had trouble discerning its truly irreducible enemies. What incited the pack against him was the apparent image of the devil, who has always been, as is known, a specialist of 'the flesh'; behind that convenient decoy, Valéry—who, in fact, *was* Lucifer—was able to give them the slip. There was no solitary

intellectual pride in Gide. A medieval inquisitor, even of the second rank, would not have been deceived for an instant."

22. See J. Hytier, *André Gide* (New York: Doubleday, 1962), pp. 67-119.

23. *Cahiers André Gide* (Paris: Gallimard, 1971), vol. 2.

24. Page references in the text to *Saül* are to *Théâtre* (Paris: Gallimard, 1942).

25. For a profound meditation on the thought of Freud, Bettelheim, and Groddeck in relation to circumcision, Judaism, and psychoanalysis, see J. Laplanche, *Problématiques* (Paris: P.U.F., 1980), vol. 2, *Castration et symbolisations*, pp. 189-311.

26. Ibid., p. 245.

27. In the *Journal* (February 1902), p. 132, Gide writes of his Biblical play in terms of understanding contemporary Jews: "Fred Natanson, returning the manuscript of *Saül* to me, feels obliged to add: 'Moreover, I've never read the Bible.' It is curious, this point of honor that all the educated Jews I know make of never having read the Bible. . . . And that allows them not to acknowledge their specific forms of ugliness [*leurs laideurs*]; yes, but they are all the more unaware of their beauties. I'll have to discuss this with Blum."

28. See A. Goulet, *Les Caves du Vatican d'André Gide* (Paris: Larousse, 1972), pp. 155-77, for a complete review of the question of Gide's "sources."

29. Bernanos, *La Grande Peur des bien-pensants: Edouard Drumont* (Paris: Grasset, 1931), pp. 209-10.

30. L. Taxil, *Pie IX Franc-maçon?* (Paris: Tequi, 1892).

31. Ibid., p. 47.

32. E. Drumont, *Le Testament d'un antisémite* (Paris: Dentu, 1892).

33. Ibid., pp. 1-2.

34. Ibid., p. 431.

35. Drumont (*Le Testament d'un antisémite*, p. 405) quotes Taxil contemptuously: "'the names of Rothschild, Pereire, Cahen d'Anvers, de Hirsch, Ephrussi, Camondo are universally esteemed.'"

36. Ibid., p. 419.

37. Ibid., p. 432.

38. There is a fierce attack against Gide's "anti-Semitism" in Modiano and Berl's *Interrogatoire*, pp. 121-22: "I cannot forgive him his stupid anti-Semitism. . . . That Gide was able to adopt exactly the same point of view as Flaubert—and that, after Freud, Einstein, Kafka, Proust, Husserl, Bergson, etc.—is absolutely incomprehensible! He doesn't abandon his position. For him, a Jew is something intermediate between Bernstein and Rothschild. There's no Durkheim! But, all the same, there was the foundation of sociology by Durkheim and Lévy-Bruhl. That is not exactly what is called selling rugs! . . . When I think that he wrote in his *Journal*, in 1914: 'I am certainly not denying the great merit of several Jewish works, say the plays of Porto-Riche, for example. But with how much lighter a heart I would admire them had they only come to us in translation. . . . For what do I care if the literature of my country is enriched, if it is to the detriment of its signification. It would be better, on the day a Frenchman no longer has sufficient energy, to disappear rather than let some ill-bred lout [*malappris*] play his role in his name and place.' This is third-rate Goebbels! I have always thought that Gide had only just barely escaped Collaboration. Things got off to a very bad start in '40, '41, but he caught himself on time. He was too prudent and too sensitive to the cold to get himself shot." There is a relatively feeble response to Berl, whose quotations are not always perfect, in *Bulletin des amis d'André Gide*, no. 34 (April 1977), "Les Citations de M. Berl," pp. 45-51.

39. His role in the novel is evoked in the *Journal* entry for 6 June 1933, p. 1173.

40. Gide, *Les Faux-monnayeurs*, p. 296.

41. See M. Pavlovic, "Lafcadio Wluiki and Guillaume Apollinaire," *Mercure de France* (April 1962), pp. 850-78.

42. It is perhaps worth remarking that one of Apollinaire's obsessions during the years of *Les Caves*'s gestation was dispelling the tenacious legend that he was Jewish. The relevant documents, including a virtual *certificat d'aryanité*, are reproduced in J. Bieder, "Quand Apollinaire se défendait d'être Juif," *Le Monde juif* (September 1947), pp. 17–19.

43. Gide, *Journal*, p. 972.

44. An example of Gide's exasperation (*Journal*, 25 May 1931, p. 1046): "I attempt to progress with the novel [*Geneviève*], without pleasure, with conviction only for the ideas I would like to promote. A detestable method. I know it; I feel it; but what can I do? And everything I write of it seems to me limp and without accent . . ."

45. *L'Ecole des femmes, Robert, Geneviève* (Paris: Gallimard, 1944), p. 179.

46. The stereotypes of Gide's evocation of the Jewess are discussed in C. Wardi, *Le Juif dans le roman français, 1933–1948* (Paris: Nizet, 1973), pp. 151–56.

47. Gide, *Geneviève*, p. 204.

48. Ibid., p. 209.

49. G. Painter, *André Gide: A Critical and Biographical Study* (London: Arthur Barker, 1951), p. 155: "Can it be that the future father of her child would have been Bernard of *The Coiners?*"

50. Sarah seems well on her way to becoming Sara in the following passage from *Les Faux-monnayeurs* (p. 282): "During her stay in England, she was able to drive her courage to the point of incandescence . . . she was resolved to conquer her freedom, to grant herself every license, to dare anything. She felt herself ready to brave every form of contempt, every accusation . . ."

51. *Journal, 1889–1939*, p. 250.

52. Blum, *Du mariage* (Paris: Ollendorff, 1907), p. 34: "'Alas, we should tell young girls that love and marriage are two different things that do not go together. They would either choose before, or they would do as you [men] do: love first and marry later.' Thus speaks the heroine of *Amoureuse*, with the intuitive capacity accorded her by a poet, and her speech, in fact, contains the whole of my argument."

53. Quoted in Lacouture, *Léon Blum*, p. 110.

54. Blum, *Du mariage*, p. 340: "But it is from the ethical point of view, not the social point of view, that I have intentionally written. My discussion is perhaps applicable to only a single class. It matters little if the solution is just, and if that class is precisely the one that has remained refractory to the ideas I have wanted to promote."

55. The rhythm of Gide's dialogue has the "first person" attacking the Jews, and Corydon responding, in essence, that such comments are beside the point. An example (*Corydon*; Paris: Gallimard, 1925, p. 115): "'Yes, I have read the book (*Du mariage*). I regard it as skillful and, consequently, rather dangerous. The Jews are past masters in the art of disintegrating our most respected and venerable institutions — the very foundations of our Western civilization — to the advantage of I know not what license and relaxation of morals which our common sense and Latin social instinct fortunately find repugnant. I have always thought that that was the most characteristic trait of their literature; of their theater, in particular.' — 'The book has been protested,' he continued, 'but by no means refuted.'"

56. Gide, *Corydon*, p. 122.

57. Gide, "La 'Plus belle histoire juive' de Gide," *Bulletin des amis d'André Gide*, no. 34 (April 1977), pp. 57–59.

58. Ibid., p. 59.

59. Ibid., p. 57.

60. A. Memmi, *Portrait d'un Juif* (Paris: Gallimard, 1962), p. 83.

61. Blum's question reminds us as well of the extent to which he was capable of figuring as a caricature himself. Thus E. Berl, *Interrogatoire*, p. 60: "Blum took advantage of his extreme myopia. He took refuge behind it and did not see what he wished not to see. That was

Proust's great reproach against him. . . . That if Blum had a lesbian as a wife and a pederast as a son, he would not have realized it. I, in fact, do not believe that he would have noticed."

62. Genet, *Notre-Dame des Fleurs* (Paris: Gallimard, 1951), p. 54.

63. Ibid., p. 52.

64. Ibid., p. 147.

65. Ibid., pp. 162–63.

66. Ibid., p. 156.

67. Derrida, *Glas* (Paris: Galilée, 1974), p. 200: "Forever on the program (oracle and good tidings), the *anthoedipe* arrives every season, like a flower."

68. Ibid., p. 267.

69. Ibid., p. 269.

Conclusion

1. For further elaboration of these concepts, see my *Revolution and Repetition: Marx/Hugo/Balzac* (Berkeley: University of California Press, 1977).

2. G. Scholem, "Redemption through Sin" in *The Messianic Idea in Judaism* (New York: Schocken, 1971), p. 126.

3. See as well his *Sabbatai Sevi: The Mystical Messiah* (Princeton: Princeton University Press, 1973). For a useful discussion of the evolution of Scholem's views on Sabbatianism, see D. Biale, *Gershom Scholem: Kabbalah and Counter-History* (Cambridge: Harvard University Press, 1979), pp. 148–70.

4. Scholem, *Major Trends in Jewish Mysticism* (New York: Schocken, 1971), p. 295.

5. Ibid., p. 297.

6. Scholem, *The Messianic Idea in Judaism*, p. 99.

7. Scholem, *Major Trends in Jewish Mysticism*, p. 308.

8. Scholem, *The Messianic Idea in Judaism*, p. 134.

9. Scholem, *Major Trends in Jewish Mysticism*, p. 320. For a biography of Frank's heir apparent, see Scholem, *Du Frankisme au jacobinisme: La vie de Moses Dobruška, alias Franz Thomas von Schönfeld alias Junius Frey* (Paris: Gallimard, Seuil, 1981).

10. Scholem, *The Messianic Idea in Judaism*, pp. 138–40.

11. Drumont, *La France Juive* (Paris: Marpon and Flammarion, 1885) vol. 1, p. 5.

12. See G. Scholem, *Walter Benjamin—die Geschichte einer Freundschaft* (Frankfurt: Suhrkamp, 1975), p. 171. Scholem notes that Benjamin was the first person to whom he communicated (in 1927) his "astonishing" discoveries—in England—concerning Sabbatian theology: "the existence of an elaborate messianic antinomianism within Judaism."

13. See Biale, *Gershom Scholem*, p. 150.

14. Benjamin, *Illuminations* (New York: Schocken, 1969), p. 254. Scholem insists at length (*Major Trends in Jewish Mysticism*, p. 293) on the personal weakness of Sabbatai Sevi, the oblivion into which all of his pronouncements have fallen.

15. Scholem, *On Jews and Judaism in Crisis* (New York: Schocken, 1976), pp. 198–236.

16. Ibid., pp. 206–7.

17. Benjamin, *Illuminations*, p. 257.

18. Scholem, *The Messianic Idea in Judaism*, p. 35: "Thus in Judaism the Messianic idea has compelled a *life lived in deferment* . . . [it] is the real anti-existentialist idea."

19. Scholem, *On Jews and Judaism in Crisis*, p. 213.

20. Benjamin, *Briefe*, ed. G. Scholem and T. Adorno (Frankfurt: Suhrkamp, 1978), vol. 2, p. 842.

21. Benjamin, *Briefe*, vol. 1, p. 219.

22. Concerning Gide, see, in addition to *Briefe*, "Gespräch mit André Gide," *Schriften*, (Frankfurt: Suhrkamp, 1974), vol. 4, p. 502; "André Gide: *La porte étroite*," vol. 2, p. 615;

"André Gide und Deutschland," vol. 4, p. 497; and "André Gide und sein neuer Gegner," vol. 3, p. 482.

23. Benjamin, *Briefe*, vol. 2, p. 753.

24. At the end of his life, as we have seen, Benjamin was faced in his work with a choice between subjects: "die Alternative Gide-Baudelaire," as he wrote (7 May 1940) to Adorno. But if Gide was suspected of seconding Céline's *Bagatelles*, Baudelaire was thought to have an even more fundamental relation to it. In the section of *Charles Baudelaire: Ein Lyriker im Zeitalter des Hochkapitalismus* called "Die Boheme," we read (*Schriften*, vol. 1, p. 516) that "the title and spirit under which Céline wrote *Bagatelles pour un massacre* recall immediately [*unmittelbar*] an entry in Baudelaire's diaries: 'A splendid conspiracy is being organized with the aim of exterminating the Jewish race.'" Of particular interest to us in the "Boheme" section is Benjamin's evocation of the *chiffonnier* (*Lumpensammler*) as exemplary Bohemian, since the *chiffonnier* in Giraudoux's Bohemia (the zanies of *La Folle de Chaillot*) was assigned the task of denouncing the race of foreign speculators invading Paris. More generally, Benjamin is interested in forging links between the Bohemians of the Second Empire ("*die Geheimniskrämerei des Verschwörers*, the mystery-mongering of the conspirator") and a problematic of representation ("*der Rätselkram der Allegorie*, the retailing of enigmas through allegory"), p. 519. I have attempted a related analysis as a reading of Marx in *Revolution and Repetition*, pp. 5–41. For a discussion of the relation between that work and Benjamin's thought, see T. Eagleton's (otherwise excellent) *Walter Benjamin or Towards a Revolutionary Criticism* (London: Verso, 1981), pp. 162-72. Both Eagleton and I regard the *Eighteenth Brumaire* as liberatory of a humor whose aesthetic potential remains to be gauged. He stops short, however, of the possibility that the dupe of the "farce" may have been Marx's dialectic itself.

25. Benjamin, *Illuminations*, p. 257.

26. Ibid., p. 264.

27. Scholem, *Walter Benjamin*, p. 200, Benjamin (*Briefe*, vol. 2, p. 505): "I can no longer hide from myself that this entire question—so long deferred—threatens to constitute one of the serious failures of my life."

28. Benjamin, *Briefe*, vol. 2, p. 506. In his Proustian *Berlin Chronicle*, Benjamin posits Paris as the medium within which he imagines the "system of signs," Berlin (*Reflections*, ed. P. Demetz, trans, E. Jephcott; New York: Harcourt Brace Jovanovich, 1979, p. 5). Even before mentioning Proust, he assigns himself "an illustrious precursor, the Frenchman Léon Daudet, exemplary at least in the title of his work which encompasses the best that I might achieve here: *Paris vécu*." That work is eloquent on the intimacy that bound the Daudets, father and son, to Drumont: "*La France juive* appeared on the stands. . . . Its success was stunning, and it was I, informed by the vendors of the galleries of the Odéon, who came to announce it to the author. Drumont's joy was something to behold . . . we drank to the health of the book that was about to positively revolutionize Paris" (*Paris vécu*; Paris: Gallimard, 1969, p. 243). One of the more unsettling legacies charted in this book would, in fact, appear to run from Drumont's *Mon vieux Paris* to Daudet's *Paris vécu* to Benjamin's *Berlin Chronicle*. (It may be noted that the allusion to Gide's Satanism in the 1938 letter to Horkheimer, previously cited, on p. 88 of this volume, immediately precedes a reference to the ignorance betrayed by Daudet in a manifestly anti-Semitic comment, *Briefe*, vol. 2, p. 753.)

29. Quoted in Scholem, *Walter Benjamin*, p. 272.

30. Scholem, *Walter Benjamin*, p. 253. Benjamin had written a short piece on Giraudoux's *Bella* ("the most beautiful realization of the art of the crossword puzzle") in 1926 (*Schriften*, vol. 3, p. 34). The most cruelly ironic comment on Benjamin's relation to Giraudoux is perhaps the latter's evocation of the flight from Paris in the wake of the Nazi invasion of France, the trip, that is, that would end in Benjamin's death. From *Sans pouvoirs* (p. 25): "June 1940: France was aroused by one of the most beautiful movements Europe has ever known."

The Exodus. It was an outburt of religion to which the Biblical name was immediately affixed. All of France, that month, decided to leave for France." The reversal of the image of Jewish triumph in this example — the Biblical Exodus — parallels the reversal of Racine's *Athalie* in *La Folle de Chaillot*.

31. Concerning Jouhandeau's anti-Semitism, see M. Marrus and R. Paxton, *Vichy et les Juifs* (Paris: Calmann-Lévy, 1981), p. 51.

32. Hannah Arendt's impression of the cemetery shortly after Benjamin's death is quoted in Scholem, *Walter Benjamin*, p. 281: "The cemetery gives onto a small bay, directly on the Mediterranean. . . . It is by far one of the most fantastic and beautiful places I have ever seen in my life."

33. Scholem, *Walter Benjamin*, p. 194. In "Qu'est-ce qu'une histoire juive?" in *La Psychanalyse est-elle une histoire juive?* (Paris: Seuil, 1981), D. Sibony relates a story exemplary of the Judaeo-analytic complex, whose bearing at this juncture makes it worth quoting: Katzmann, wanting to Gallicize his name, changes it to *Chat* (=Katz)-*l'homme* (=mann), that is: *Shalom*, the Hebrew salutation. For Sibony, Judaism begins in this kind of linguistic — or onomastic — malaise.

34. Luria's Kabbalah is the theological basis of Harold Bloom's *Kabbalah and Criticism* (New York: Seabury, 1975). The distinctions elaborated in this conclusion may provide a context for understanding Bloom's rather willful swipes at recent French thought: "More audacious than any developments in recent French criticism, Kabbalah is a theory of *writing*, but this is a theory that denies the absolute distinction between writing and inspired speech . . ." (p. 52).

35. Eagleton, in *Walter Benjamin*, p. 10, has analyzed Benjamin's book on *Trauerspiel* in terms of the "leakage of meaning from objects, the unhinging of signifiers from signifieds . . ."

36. Scholem, *The Messianic Idea in Judaism*, p. 110.

37. Scholem, *On Jews and Judaism in Crisis*, p. 210.

38. The French translator of "The Work of Art in the Age of Mechanical Reproduction" had been Pierre Klossowski, leading contributor to the College. On Benjamin's relations with the members of the College, see D. Hollier's invaluable *Le Collège de Sociologie (1937-1939)* (Paris: Gallimard, 1979).

39. Bataille, *L'Erotisme* (Paris: Minuit, 1957), p. 70. For a provocative discussion of Bataille's thought on transgression as a matrix for future speculation, see M. Foucault, "Préface à la transgression" in *Critique* 195-96 (August-September 1963), pp. 751-69.

40. Scholem, *The Messianic Idea in Judaism*, p. 99.

Appendix I. Black Gracq

1. I would like to acknowledge my debt to the rich collection of materials assembled by J.-L. Leutrat in *Julien Gracq*, a special issue of *L'Herne*, the title of whose liminary essay, "A Noir," quoted from Rimbaud's "Voyelles," my own (half-)translates.

2. Gracq's novels are *Au Chateau d'Argol* (1938), *Un Beau ténébreux* (1945), *Le Rivage des Syrtes* (1951), and *Un Balcon en forêt* (1958). In addition, he has published a volume of Rimbaldian prose poems, *Liberté grande* (1947), an unsuccessful play, *Le Roi pêcheur* (1948), a collection of critical texts, *Préférences* (1961), three volumes of reflections, *Lettrines* (1967, 1974) and *En lisant en écrivant* (1981), a triptych of short *récits*, *La Presqu'île* (1970), and a long essay, *Les Eaux étroites* (1976). José Corti is the publisher of all these works.

3. See my "A propos du mot *unheimlich* chez Marx" in *Critique* 333 (February 1975). An English version of that essay serves as chapter 1 of my *Revolution and Repetition: Marx/Hugo/Balzac* (Berkeley: University of California Press, 1977).

4. *Der achtzehnte Brumaire des Louis Bonaparte* in Marx, *Werke* (Berlin: Dietz Verlag, 1960), vol. 8, p. 161.

5. Gracq, *Lettrines*, p. 139.

6. See Gracq, *Lettrines*, p. 68: "Nothing attains the hauteur of tone, the precision of shot —which courses straight through, without even drawing blood – the savage gaiety of Marx the journalist."

7. Gracq, *Lettrines*, p. 57.

8. Gracq, *Lettrines*, vol. 2, p. 111.

9. Gracq, *Lettrines*, p. 29.

10. Gracq, *Un Beau ténébreux*, p. 52.

11. Gracq, *Au Chateau d'Argol*, p. 56.

12. Ibid., p. 61.

13. Ibid., p. 67.

14. Ibid., p. 74.

15. Gracq, *Les Eaux étroites* (Paris: Corti, 1976), p. 27.

16. Gracq, *Lettrines*, vol. 2., p. 6.

17. Ibid., p. 8.

18. Ibid., p. 84.

19. Ibid., p. 85.

20. Jean-Paul Weber, in *Domaines thématiques* (Paris: Gallimard, 1963), organizes his reading of Gracq around a recollection, by the author, of the launching of the Ile-de-France. Gracq, in *Préférences*, p. 62: "Perhaps there is always still in the background that image from my youth, a sliding without return: the launching of an enormous ship."

21. Mallarmé, *Oeuvres complètes* (Paris: Pléiade, 1961), pp. 541–46. The ultimate failure Mallarmé ascribes to Wagner is, of course, complicated by the fact that Mallarmé's aesthetic is ultimately one *of* failure.

22. Hemorrhage appears to be the medium within which history transpires in Gracq. Thus, of Chateaubriand: "In order to find later on that toneless voice [*cette voix blanche*], one corresponding to large losses of blood, that pallor of the forehead, rustling of dead leaves, the accent of a chilly, erratic, autumnal religiosity, the literature of the Russian Revolution would have to wait until *Doctor Zhivago*" (*Préférences*, p. 156). Of *time* in Racine's *Bajazet*: "a concentrated tension, an urgency which causes the hours and minutes to resemble blood pulsating out of an open vein" (*Préférences*, p.201).

23. See R. M. Albérès, *Esthétique et morale chez Jean Giraudoux* (Paris: Nizet, 1970), p. 338. The single act of the uncomplete play has been published in *La Menteuse suivi de Les Gracques* (Paris: Grasset, 1958).

24. See C. Nicolet, *Les Gracques: Crise agraire et Révolution à Rome* (Paris: Julliard, 1967), p. 202: "Tiberius' sole crime, in the eyes of the Senate, had been to attack the precautions and mechanisms which had hitherto prevented the *populus* from expressing massively and simply its opinion. Like all oligarchical republics . . . the Roman republic feared the direct exercise of sovereignty, and, consequently, the vote. It possessed an extremely complicated system of successive instances, of votes grouped by property-holding or geographical categories, or by age, which locked the individual into his context, diluted his voice, and bridled his initiative."

25. *La Presqu'île*, published in 1970, consists of three short stretches of fiction and is in no sense a novel.

26. Gracq, "Sur *Un Balcon en forêt*," in *Julien Gracq* (Paris: L'Herne, n.d.), p. 214.

27. Guardians of the wood/Guardians rather of sleep/Watch at least for the dawn.

28. Gracq, *Un Balcon en forêt*, p. 146.

29. Ibid., pp. 168, 228.

30. Ibid., p. 246.

31. Ibid., p. 253.

32. Gracq, *Le Roi pêcheur*, p. 35.

33. Ibid., p. 31.

34. Ibid., p. 17.

35. Gracq, *Un Balcon en forêt*, p. 167.

36. Ibid., p. 44.

37. Gracq, *Le Rivage des Syrtes*, p. 274. See G. Deleuze, *Nietzsche et la philosophie* (Paris: P.U.F., 1967), p. 10: "The extreme enjoyment [*jouissance*] of difference, that is the new, aggressive, aerial element that empiricism substitutes for the ponderous notions of dialectic."

38. Gracq, *Un Balcon en forêt*, p. 211.

39. Curiously enough, the concrete experience of going – drunk – beyond the German lines as a French soldier had none of this intensity. See "La nuit des ivrognes" in *Lettrines*, pp. 120-26.

40. Gracq, "L'oeuvre de Ernst Jünger en France" in *L'Herne*, p. 205. George Steiner writes of Jünger's literary record of his Occupation of France in *Language and Silence* (Atheneum: New York, 1977), p. 105: "Jünger wrote an account of the victorious campaign in France. It is a lyric, elegant little book, entitled *Gärten und Strassen*. Not a rude note in it. An old-style officer taking fatherly care of his French prisoners and entertaining 'correct' and even gracious relations with his new subjects. Behind his staff car come the trucks of the Gestapo and the elite guards fresh from Warsaw. Jünger does not mention any such unpleasantness. He writes of gardens."

41. Gracq, *Préférences*, p. 23.

42. Gracq, *L'Herne*, p. 219.

43. Gracq, *Préférences*, p. 101.

44. Gracq, *Lettrines*, vol. 2, p. 70.

45. Gracq, *Un Balcon en forêt*, p. 242.

46. Gracq, *Préférences*, p. 247.

47. Gracq, *Les Eaux étroites*, pp. 30-31.

48. Jünger, *Strahlungen* (Tübingen: Heliopolis-Verlag, 1949), p. 27.

49. Jünger, *Sur les falaises de marbre* (Paris: Gallimard, 1942), pp. 18-19.

50. Ibid., p. 190.

51. For the dissemination of this chain, and indeed for the general context of these remarks, see Derrida, *Glas* (Paris: Galilée, 1974), as well as my *Revolution and Repetition*.

52. Gracq's one translation from the German is Kleist's *Penthesilea*. His preface has Kleist's German drawing on the "oriental aspect of the Greek genius," in contact with "monstrous forms emergent from the East" (p. 16). The fantasmatics of, say, Farghestan were part and parcel of the act of translating, for the strangeness of the play was inherently linked to its foreignness ("a masterpiece perhaps, but in that case in the full sense of the word *un chef d'oeuvre étrange – un chef d'oeuvre étranger*," p. 11). Gracq ends his preface by evoking Kleist's disdainful presentation of his play: "It may be recalled how Kleist tendered it to the public, with a rather *distant* finger, 'This evening, by special permission, *Penthesilea*, a canine play. Characters: heroes, mongrels, women.'" The Germanic distance of Kleist was evoked as the "distinctive merit" of Jünger ("I would say that his merit, on the contrary, lies in the *distance* that an almost inhuman, mineral style – in which, it may almost be said, language, in its density, crystallizes according to its enigmatic molecular laws rather than the will of the writer – interposes between the act of observation and the thing observed," *Préférences*, p. 251). But more relevant still is the designation "canine play." For Jünger's swarm of glyphic serpents enveloping to the point of indistinction the pack of dogs in the sequence of *Les Falaises* we have examined would then offer an image of a relation to Germany that both informs his fiction – reinscription of *la bande* – and *orients* his efforts as translator.

53. The text was subsequently republished as *Zur Seinsfrage* (Frankfurt: Klostermann, 1956).

54. See Derrida's *"La Double Séance"* in *La Dissémination* (Paris: Seuil, 1972), as well as my "Mallarmé/Maxwell: Elements," *Romanic Review* (Fall, 1981).

55. Note that in Aldo's meditation, in *Le Rivage des Syrtes*, on the line of demarcation, the passage *across* the line glides into a journey *along the line*: "in allowing my eyes so often to slide in a kind of total conviction along that red thread, like a bird entranced by a line traced before it on the earth, it had ended up being permeated for me with a kind of bizarre reality: without my being willing to admit it to myself, I was ready to attribute to that perilous passage concrete wonders, to imagine a crevice in the sea, a warning signal, the crossing of the *Red Sea* . . . " (p. 34). The sequence prepares the eventual crossing of the Line and bespeaks its fascination. It is remarkable, then, that the same image of the bird informs an *abdication* from transgression in *Le Roi pêcheur*. Amfortas: "There are birds one can put to sleep by making them stare at a white line, and there exists behind every act a wake [*sillage*], a trace which grows, and if one stares at it long enough, a dizziness descends on you that will capsize your heart, and which nevertheless possesses a charm, since it entrances. Thus did Montsalvage fall asleep midst its branches, like a ship on the waves . . ." (p. 98). The farther the move *trans lineam* [*über die Linie*] is pressed, the more does one enter into a topology *de linea*.

56. The logic of the *bande* or inland coast governs the opening of *Liberté grande* ("*Pour galvaniser l'urbanisme*"). Once its vessels are cut ("streaming with a keen black asphalt blood at each of its slashed arteries . . ."), the City of Paris itself becomes a vessel ("the fantastic vision of the vessel of Paris ready to cast off its moorings for a voyage to the very bottom of dreams") taking off for a sea voyage on dry land: "on an ocean of *green-meadow*, better executed than nature." Split in the vessel, and constitution of a *bande*: thus do Gracq's prose poems begin.

INDEX OF NAMES

INDEX OF NAMES

Abraham, K., 23, 119
Adorno, T., 131
Alain, 117
Alain-Fournier, 43
Albérès, R. M., 134
Amouroux, H., 117
Andreu, P., 9, 115
Apollinaire, G., 77, 129, 130
Aragon, L., 35, 123
Arendt, H., 133
Arland, M., 128
Auerbach, E., 120

Bakan, D., 119, 121
Barrès, M., 114, 127
Barthes, R., 113
Bataille, G., 15-16, 90, 133
Baudelaire, C., 132
Béguin, A., 120
Bénézet, M., 107-9
Benjamin, W., 83, 86-90, 131-33
Bentham, J., 17, 19
Bergson, H., 13, 124
Berl, E., 127, 129, 130-31
Bernanos, G., 6-7, 8, 9, 10, 16, 18-21, 25, 46, 73, 75, 83, 113, 115, 116, 118, 119, 120, 125, 129
Bernays, I., 31-32
Bernays, M., 31-32
Bernstein, H., 39-40, 124
Bettelheim, B., 129
Biale, D., 131
Bieder, J., 130
Billy, A., 43

Blanchot, M., 3, 6-22, 63, 83, 107-9, 113, 114-19, 123, 127
Bloom, H., 133
Bloy, L., 23-33, 83, 119-23
Blum, L., 10, 11, 65, 78-80, 108, 127, 129, 130-31
Body, J., 44, 123, 124
Bonaparte, M., 123
Borges, J. L., 120
Borinsky, A., 118
Brasillach, R., 45, 52, 113, 124

Céline, L.-F., 4, 21, 35, 64, 65, 88, 108, 113, 119, 127, 128, 132
Chateaubriand, F. R., vicomte de, 134
Claudel, P., 117, 119, 128
Clavel, M., 6, 20, 118-19
Clemenceau, G., 7
Colette, G.-S., 39-40
Copeau, J., 67
Curtius, E. R., 117-18

Daudet, L., 64, 115, 127, 132
Deleuze, G., 13, 116, 135
Derrida, J., 17, 330, 82, 87, 115, 121, 131, 135, 136
Desanti, D., 120
Dioudonnat, P.-M., 124
Dresden, D., 115
Dreyfus, A., 114
Drieu la Rochelle, P., 8, 44, 56, 113, 117, 119-20, 122
Driver, S. R., 125
Drumont, E., 6-7, 8, 18-21, 25-26, 64, 72-

INDEX

76, 86, 108, 113, 114, 118, 120, 127, 129, 132

Druon, M., 54

Dubech, L., 40

Eagleton, T., 132, 133

Fabre-Luce, A., 113
Fabrègues, J. de, 115
Farrère, C., 40
Flandin, P.-E., 11
Foucault, M., 6, 13, 17, 18-21, 116, 118, 120, 125, 133
France, A., 19
Franco, F., 9
Frank, J., 85-86
Fresnois, A. du, 43-44, 124
Freud, E., 31, 122
Freud, S., 4-5, 23-33, 55, 84, 119-23, 129

Genet, J., 81-82, 131
Gide, A., 3, 39, 64-82, 83, 87-88, 113, 117, 124, 127-31, 132, 133
Gilbert, P., 124
Giraudoux, J., 3, 34-63, 83, 89, 98, 113, 118, 123-27, 132, 134
Glucksmann, A., 18-21, 118
Gobineau, J. A., comte de, 40
Goulet, A., 129
Gracq, J., 92-106, 128-29, 133-36
Graetz, H., 86
Groddeck, G., 129
Guillemin, H., 115

Hegel, G. W. F., 22, 30, 82
Heidegger, M., 17, 105-5
Hitler, A., 3, 7, 9, 11, 16, 43, 45, 47, 62, 113, 114
Hollier, D., 117, 133
Horkheimer, M., 88, 132
Horowitz, I. L., 115, 116
Hugo, V., 41
Hytier, J., 129

Jammes, F., 128
Jarry, A., 76-77
Jouhandeau, M., 89, 133
Jouvenel, B. de, 115
Jouvet, L., 56, 126
Jünger, E., 101-6, 135

Jurt, J., 114

Klee, P., 86-88, 90
Kleist, H. von, 135
Kline, T. J., 125
Klossowski, P., 133

Lacan, J., 3, 7, 23-33, 83, 113, 119-23, 128
Laclos, C. de, 36, 37, 38, 58
Lacouture, J., 127
Laplanche, J., 126, 129
Laubreaux, A., 124
Léautaud, P., 117
Lessing, G., 32
Lestringuez, P., 58
Leutrat, J.-L., 133
Lévinas, 16-18, 19, 118
Lévy, B.-H., 107, 114
Loewenstein, R., 29, 121
Loubet del Bayle, J.-L., 115

Mallarmé, S., 30, 94-95, 98, 99, 106, 134, 136
Mandel, G., 11, 116
Maritain, J., 64, 65, 88, 127
Marrus, M., 54, 113, 126, 133
Marx, K., 13, 93-94, 132, 133, 134
Maulnier, T., 8, 14-15, 16, 115, 118
Mauriac, F., 70, 117
Mauron, C., 36-37, 41, 48-49, 52, 53, 54, 57, 123, 125, 126
Maurras, C., 8, 44, 114, 115, 124, 128
Mauss, M., 82
Memmi, A., 80, 130
Mille, P., 40
Modiano, P., 113, 127, 129
Montesquieu, C.-L. de S., baron de, 39
Montherlant, H. de, 12-13, 14, 15, 124
Morand, P., 43, 124
Morès, marquis de, 7, 115
Morize, A., 123
Moutote, D., 128
Mussolini, B., 9

Natanson, F., 129
Nicolet, C., 134
Nietzsche, F., 15, 84, 100, 135

Painter, G., 128, 130
Pascal, B., 22, 38
Paulhan, J., 12-13, 15, 21, 22, 115, 117

INDEX

Pavlovic, M., 129
Paxton, R., 113, 114, 126, 133
Péguy, C., 8, 45
Pétain, P., 14, 127
Poliakov, L., 4, 114, 115
Pontalis, J.-B., 126
Porto-Riche, G. de, 78, 129
Primo de Rivera, J. A., 9
Proudhon, Cercle, 8, 13, 44-45, 46, 51,
    115, 116, 124
Proust, M., 67-70, 76, 80, 83, 97-98, 128,
    131

Rabelais, F., 20
Racine, J., 3, 14-15, 34-63, 83, 118, 134
Rancière, D., 118
Rancière, J., 118
Rank, O., 121
Raymond, A., 123
Rebatet, L., 40, 56, 113, 116, 124
Renan, E., 6
Riffaterre, M., 30, 121
Rimbaud, A., 13
Robert, M., 119
Robichez, J., 123, 124
Rousseau, J.-J., 53, 87
Roy, C., 113, 115, 116, 124

Saint-Simon, L. de R., duc de, 69
Sarraut, A., 11
Sartre, J.-P., 28-29, 63, 82, 113, 121,
    127

Schlumberger, J., 117
Schoen, E., 87
Scholem, G., 5, 84-90, 114, 131-33
Schorske, C. E., 119
Sérant, P., 115
Sevi, Sabbatai, 84-86, 131
Sibony, D., 133
Sorel, G., 7, 8, 13, 44, 51, 115, 116
Steiner, G., 114, 135
Sternhell, Z., 114, 115, 120, 124
Strauss, L., 123

Taine, H., 6, 86
Taxil, L., 73-76, 129
Tertullian, 120
Thomas, H., 101
Tolstoy, L., 102
Toussenel, A. de, 64, 127
Truffaut, F., 124

Vacher de Lapouge, G., 4, 114
Valéry, P., 4, 114, 117, 128-29
Vallès, J., 8, 93-94
Valois, G., 124
Vildrac, C., 113
Voltaire, F.-M. A. de, 19

Wagner, R., 96, 98, 99-101, 103, 104, 105,
    106, 134
Wardi, C., 113, 130
Weber, J.-P., 134
Winckelmann, J. J., 24, 119

Jeffrey Mehlman, an associate professor of French at Boston University, has taught at Cornell, Johns Hopkins, and the University of California. He is the author of *A Structural Study of Autobiography: Proust, Leiris, Sartre, Levi-Strauss*; *Revolution and Repetition: Marx/Hugo/Balzac*; and *Cataract: A Study in Diderot*. He wrote *Legacies* while holding a Guggenheim Fellowship.